THE SACRED PATH TO ISLAM

The Sincere Seeker

TABLE OF CONTENTS:

INTRODUCTION

In the name of Allah, the Most Compassionate, Most Merciful. All praises are due to Allah; we praise Him; we seek His Help; we seek His Forgiveness, and we seek His Guidance. We seek refuge in Allah from the evil in our souls and the wickedness of our deeds. For whoever Allah Guides, there is none to lead him astray. And for whoever He allows to go astray, there is none to guide him. I bear witness that there is none worthy of worship except Allah, for whom there is no partner. And I bear witness that Muhammad is His servant and last and final Messenger.

The work I present here for your consumption is more than a book; a collection of words meant to deliver glad tidings, to educate, and to perhaps warn. It is a work driven by what I intend to be a sound and powerful Message.

This message invites readers to think freely and broaden their minds; to contemplate and seek their own truth. This passage advises people, never to blindly follow any religion without first reflecting upon the faith in question and reasoning its true meaning. This passage encourages readers to think about, reflect upon, and understand their own collection of spiritual beliefs. Beyond all manner of faith and feeling, one must use their intellect to discover the truth behind all faiths.

This passage is intended to draw and empower the sincere seeker of truth; the one that questions, reflects and ponders his or her life's purpose and questions his/her future and direction.

Islam, for example, is one faith that is misunderstood and misrepresented by many. Before one forms an opinion of Islam, one should question the thoroughness and truthfulness of his or her existing knowledge of this controversial religion.

Has this knowledge been drawn from and formed through third-party sources that are non-Muslim in origin? Has this information been obtained through the popular media? In fairness to the religion and to one's self, one's opinion of Islam should be formed only after a careful study of the religion's original and primary sources: The Holy Quran and the teachings of humanity's final Prophet, Muhammad peace be upon him.

The ultimate purpose of this message is to facilitate a fresh new dimension of thinking that will enable one to realize the ultimate importance of his or her existence in this universe; to help one understand his/her divine relationship with his/her creator. The faith of Islam is beneficial only to people that are sincere in seeking guidance, misguiding those who are not sincere and honest in their spiritual quests; who reject divine guidance and spiritual truth.

Before you proceed, please ask yourself, 'What is my intention in reading this book?'

May your journey to the answer, and the truth be pleasant and successful

ABOUT THIS BOOK & VISION

Do you seek to know the true Message and Wisdom of Islam? Do you yearn to build a closer and more meaningful relationship with your Creator? This book is intended to serve those seeking God and the Truth, new converts to the Islamic faith, and current Muslims both practicing and non-practicing.

When I initiated my study of the Holy Quran, I was awestruck by its inimitable style, peerless form, and powerful spiritual impact. It fascinated me to discover that it contained and conveyed signs of God's Greatness, miracles, parables, and lessons for me and humanity as a whole. It amazed me to learn that the Holy Quran deals with all the subjects which concern me and people of today; including doctrine, wisdom, worship, law, transactions, and more. I could very much relate to this Book, finding in its pages answers to issues I had encountered throughout my life. The more time I spent reading this Book, the more it helped me discover myself.

As I studied the Holy Quran more deeply, I was left mesmerized by its structure, power, cohesiveness, Wisdom, spiritual elevation, and the language it uses. The more I read the Holy Quran and studied Islam, the closer I felt to God; the more I loved Him. Islam and the Holy Quran introduced me to an entity who is All-Loving, All-Knowledgeable, All-Hearing, All-Seeing. It introduced me to my Lord, the Creator of this World and all it contains. It introduced me to a God that established the path to self-transformation, and Whose laws only lighten the burdens in my life. It fascinated me.

I developed the urge to share with others the Message of this incredible Book and its inherent religion. I want to introduce people to the Religion of Islam in a unique, authentic, academic, engaging, spiritual, and fun way; thus, inspiring them to morally, intellectually, and spiritually lead more fulfilling lives in this world, and to be better prepared for the next life. Taking the journey of Islam will change a person for the better, providing them a meaning and a purpose in their life.

The concept behind writing this book is first to please God the Almighty.

Many people experience a deep depression that stems from their inner emptiness, and a keen spiritual disconnection from God. This is a normal feeling that affects nearly everyone. This book aims to enlighten people knowing that the real source of happiness and contentment stems from the pure faith in God; that pure, genuine, and unbendable faith which leads people to worship and serve Him alone.

This book seeks to connect people to the best Book that ever existed. A Divine Book designed to guide humanity and lead them to a better life in this world and the hereafter. The Holy Quran is not just another book, it is a unique Book that transforms the way one thinks, feels, and lives. Islam and the Holy Quran changes people from within and makes them better people. The Holy Qur'an is like no other book, as it stands as an infinite source of intellectual wisdom and spiritual elevation.

The goal is to help people find the Wisdom, Inspiration, and Beauty in Islam and The Holy Quran. For many Muslims, Islam is about laws, regulations do's and don'ts. Many people are not adequately educated about Allah's words, Wisdom, Advise, and develop a feeling and assumption that God is a harsh, stern, cruel, demanding God who commands people to respect Him, worship Him, and obey Him fully, and is not loving and kind to His creation. Nothing could be further from the truth. God is All-Loving; All-Merciful. Islam is far more than just a set of rules and regulations. The Sincere Seeker aims to help people realize that Islam is full of wisdom, love, and mercy to all.

Everyone is encouraged to visit the various posts and videos featured on The Sincere Seeker Blog on https://www.thesincereseeker.com or on The Sincere Seeker's YouTube Channel. People are also encouraged to subscribe to The

Sincere Seeker newsletter and YouTube Channel, to be notified when a new post or video is available for review.

For questions or comments, contact The Sincere Seeker at
hello@thesincereseeker.com

ABOUT ME?

It's important to note I am not a scholar of the religion of Islam nor do I have any official diplomas in religious studies or Islamic Studies. I developed The Sincere Seeker platform and wrote this book in my spare time after graduating with a secular degree in the United States. My feeble contribution is not comparable to those of Islam's more learned and knowledgeable scholars. My intention to creating The Sincere Seeker Platform and writing this book is to use some of my skills to contribute to society and to teach others about Allah (Glorified and Exalted be he), The Holy Quran, and the Religion and way of life of Islam in a different approach.

RELIGION OF ISLAM

Islam is the voluntary 'submission' or 'surrender' to the Will of God, in exchange for the acquisition of peace and contentment in this life and the hereafter. The Religion of Islam teaches and encourages one to submit to the will of God, in exchange to gain peace & contentment. The word Islam is the synonym of the noun *'aslama'* which means 'resigned or submitted.' In the context of religion, it means, 'to submit one's will, to the will of God.' The Religion of Islam encourages one to submit to the will of God, in exchange to acquire peace and contentment in this life and the hereafter. Only when one submits to God, by believing in Him and obeying His commandments, does one achieve an innate and lasting sense of security, true peace of mind, and surety of heart.

The word 'Islam' is derived from an Arabic root word which means peace, purity, safety, salutation, submission, acceptance, surrender, and obedience. With the act of submission, one would attain peace within themselves, and in accordance with their Creator and their fellow beings. The religion of Islam demonstrates that only through the doing of good and the seeking of God's pleasure can one find true happiness, peace, and contentment in life.

Man cannot live peacefully or successfully without religion, and this religion cannot be man-made. Religion has to be utterly Divine, with no human alteration. The only Revelation in the world today that still rings good and true is the final Book, the last and final Testament of God, The Holy Quran. All other traditional Revelations were lost in the annals of time or underwent endless human-made modifications that rendered them impractical for humanity.

Islam is a monotheistic religion; a faith in which followers admit and recognize the existence of one Supreme God and Being who is Almighty, All-Powerful, All-Knowledgeable, All-Loving. Islam stresses only One God. The same God of Prophet Adam, Noah, Abraham, Joseph, Moses, David, Solomon, Jesus, and Prophet Muhammad peace be upon them all. Islam demonstrates the fact that, through the centuries, God has continued to bless humanity with holy Prophets who come bearing the same general message.

The message is simple: one should worship God Alone with no partners, love Him with all his or her heart, and follow His Commandments. God is an entity worthy of worship, veneration, adoration, and reverence since He is the creator of everything. No other being is worthy of worship. This has always been God's Message to mankind, as conveyed through the words of Prophets and Messengers.

Prophet Moses peace be upon him declared to the people of Israel: *'Hear, O Israel; The Lord our God is one Lord' (Deuteronomy 6:4).* A full 1500 years later, Prophet Jesus peace be upon him repeated the same Message to the people of Israel: *'The first of all the commandments is, 'Hear, O Israel; the Lord our God is one Lord' (Mark 12:29).* Finally, 600 years later, Prophet Muhammad peace be upon him called out across the hills of Mecca:

> **"And your God is one God. There is no deity [worthy of worship] except Him, the Beneficent, the Especially Merciful" (Quran 2:163)**

Throughout history, anyone who practiced monotheism by submitting to the will of God and following his prophet was considered a Muslim. Human beings have been practicing Islam since the creation of Prophet Adam. Throughout the ages, God sent Prophets and Messengers to guide and teach their nations. All Prophets preached the same general Message to their nations. Muslim believe the Prophets preached that submitting to God would bring one peace and contentment to one's heart in this world; and would award on the attainment of God's kingdom and grace in the next world. No other is worthy of worship; not the Sun, the Moon, nor an idol.

Contrary to popular belief, Islam is not a new religion that came into existence 1400 years ago, back in the 7th century. Islam has existed since the first moment that man set foot on the earth.

"Truly, the religion with Allah is Islam (submission to Him)" (Quran 3:19)

Islam is the only religion that God ever commanded humankind to follow. Islam, therefore, is the only religion that has ever been acceptable to and ordained by God. Allah states in the Quran:

"And whoever seeks a religion other than Islam, it will never be accepted of him, and in the Hereafter, he will be one of the losers" (Quran 3:85)

The final Prophet of mankind, Prophet Muhammad, was not the founder of Islam, as many people mistakenly think. Instead, he was sent as the last and final Prophet; one delivered from the hand of Almighty God to convey His message to our nation, the final nation.

Islam is not a religion solely based on creeds, customs, and rituals; rather, Islam is a complete way of life that guides man in every field and aspect of this sometimes-perilous existence. Islam teaches the art of living; how one should steer and navigate his or her life. Islam instructs us about the things in this life beneficial to us, and that which is ultimately destructive and should be avoided.

Islam guides followers in every aspect of their lives. Islam emphasizes how the belief in God empowers one to become more righteous, obedient, moral, and ethical overall; rejecting all forms of evil. Islam changes a person's thoughts, actions, and life perspective; helping them to see this world as it is, and to prepare for the afterlife.

Muslims believe Islam neither neglects the needs, wants, hopes, and aspirations of this worldly life; nor does it abandon the preparation needed to ready oneself for the hereafter where man shall live eternally. Islam takes the middle path. It is better for one to ponder deeply about his or her future, and to live a good life in anticipation of his/her future eternal life. Each person is expected to devote some time to his present life to ponder what will occur in the life to come.

Islam is a religion based on faith, love, compassion, peace, mercy, goodwill, and ethical treatment to all of God's creations including humankind, animals, and plants. Islam is a religion based on self-righteousness, in which Muslims strive to perform good deeds toward the attainment of their salvation, and the goal of entering Heaven with God's Mercy in the afterlife.

A person that submits his or her will to Almighty God and follows His commandments is called a Muslim. A Muslim is one who does not follow his desires, lusts, and impulses. A Muslim is one that does right, stands for good, and loves God with all his or her heart. The act of knowing and loving God is the only thing that can bring about true contentment in the soul. If one does not have a relationship with his Creator, his soul will always seek something to fill the emptiness in his or her heart. All the wealth and material goods of this world could never be able to fill the emptiness and gap of a vacant soul. Happiness is not derived from the gathering of possessions. Real wealth is obtained only from the richness and contentment of the heart and soul. And the only true poverty is the poverty of the spirit and heart.

Islam answers the fundamental questions that malign the conscience of every human being. Why was I created? What am I doing here? What is the purpose of my existence? Islam delivers a meaningful purpose to one's life in this world; and the guidance needed to fulfill one's life purpose.

Other religions do not answer the big questions of life, such as 'Who made us?' 'Why are we here?' and 'Where are we headed?' Man cannot live peacefully in this world without knowing who he is, who has created him, where he is headed, what his role is, and how to fulfill that role to the best of his or her ability. The need to answer these questions has been implanted in man's inner nature by the Almighty. However, the human intellect alone cannot answer these questions unaided. Muslims believe Man needs Divine guidance to discover these all-important spiritual answers. The answers lie in Islam.

Islam teaches people that they were created to worship God and that the basis of all true worship is God-consciousness; a concept that includes the fear of God, the love of God, His recognition, piety, and loyalty. Since Islam encompasses all aspects of life and ethics, God-consciousness is encouraged in the execution of all human affairs.

Islamic worship is not limited to religious rituals such as praying and fasting. Instead, Islam clarifies that everyday human acts such as eating, drinking, greeting others, sitting, learning, dressing, sleeping, giving charity, are all acts of worship if done for God alone and in accordance with His Divine Laws and guidelines. The teachings of the Holy Quran and Prophet Muhamad peace be upon him can supply both ethereal mercy and a healing for the human soul. They provide the ultimate guidance for leading a productive, successful life. Islam demonstrates the best way of living a life.

God created man to be a follower and a worshipper. If he is not devoted to God, he will devote himself to others; whether they are false gods, saints, idols, philosophers, etc., following them by thoughts and actions that would lead him astray. In Islam, Muslims do not worship the creations of God, such as the sun, the moon, or an idol; instead, they worship the Creator Himself. Islam recognizes that God has created humans with an innate eagerness and ability to seek God, to acknowledge and understand the existence of their Creator.

The highest and most significant thinkers of the past never would deny the various signs that point to the existence of their Creator. However, what led many people of the past astray is the lack of knowing God properly and the fact they did not have access to a true and preserved Revelation originating from God. Aimed at the ones that deny God's existence, God poses an argument in the Quran stating:

"Or were they created by nothing, or were they the creators [of themselves]?" "Or did they create the heavens and the earth? Rather, they are not certain" (Quran 52:35-36)

The aim of these verses is for mankind to reflect and ponder on the fact they could not have come into existence from nothing, nor could they have created themselves. In another Verse, God states the skies and the Earth are fashioned perfectly, hence showing proof they were originated from the act of a Creator.

"Indeed, in the creation of the heavens and earth, and the alternation of the night and the day, and the [great] ships which sail through the sea with that which benefits people, and what Allah has sent down from the heavens of rain, giving life thereby to the earth after its lifelessness and dispersing therein every [kind of] moving creature, and [His] directing of the winds and the clouds controlled between the heaven and the earth are signs for a people who use reason" (Quran 2:164)

The miracles of nature, the Earth, the Universe are enough evidence to show mankind that there is 'something bigger than us.' Humanity does not need God to show them anything more for them to believe; the world is already enough of a miracle.

"It is He who sends down rain from the sky; from it is drink and from it is foliage in which you pasture [animals]. He causes to grow for you the crops, olives, palm trees, grapevines, and from all the fruits. In that is a sign for a people who give thought. And He has subjected for you the night and day and the sun and moon, and the stars are subjected by His command. In that are signs for a people who reason. And [He has subjected] whatever He multiplied for you on the earth of varying colors. Indeed, in that is a sign for a people who remember. And it is He who subjected the sea for you to eat from it tender meat and to extract from it ornaments which you wear. And you see the ships plowing through it, and [He subjected it] that you may seek of His bounty; and perhaps you will be grateful. And He has cast into the earth firmly set mountains, lest it shift with you, and [made] rivers and roads, that you may be guided, And landmarks. And by the stars they are [also] guided. Then is He who creates like one who does not create? So, will you not be reminded?" (Quran 16:10-17)

Surely these words will answer the questions and address the doubts of people who ponder, people who think, people who reflect.

The Religion of Islam states that God forces no one to submit to His Will. He has laid out a clear path for human beings while making it known that humans must choose from two routes: The straight path that leads to Heaven, or the erroneous way which leads to hell. Human beings are free to make their own choices. Islam forces no one to submit. A human who worships God, pledging their devotion to Him and obeying His commands, has grasped the firm handhold and eternal bond that will never break. Whoever denies God's existence or worships anyone other than Allah, stands to face eternal punishment in the hereafter.

Life is a test of one's faith. God the Almighty, out of his abundant Love and Mercy for humanity, has not left us in pure darkness; leaving us alone and unenlightened to discover the right path through the frailties of guesswork or trial and error.

God gifted mankind with an intellect and a logical mind that can reason, ponder, and reflect. God bestowed upon humanity the gift of Divine Guidance, that outlines the Criterion for ultimate truth and knowledge.

One is expected to use his or her intellect and reason to contemplate and recognize God's signs, to build a relationship with Him, and to follow His guidance. These signs serve to speak loudly, without the need of talking to God directly, which would then not require any effort or reflection by the human.

"Whoever does righteousness, whether male or female, while he is a believer - We will surely cause him to live a good life, and We will surely give them their reward [in the Hereafter] according to the best of what they used to do" (Quran 16:97)

The disbelievers, the rejecters of the truth, the deniers of God, will live a narrow, depressed life in this world and abide in hellfire forever in the hereafter.

"And whoever turns away from My remembrance - indeed, he will have a depressed life, and We will gather him on the Day of Resurrection blind" (Quran 20:124)

The goal of Islam is for the one to become a faithful servant of God. Judgment Day is a blink away. You live, and you die, and then you will inevitably be resurrected to face your Lord, who will judge you based on the way you lived your life.

"...Indeed, we belong to Allah, and indeed to Him, we will return"
(Quran 2:156)

GOD (ALLAH)

The word 'Allah' is the unique name of God. He is The One and Only, the Absolute & Eternal God. He is the creator of the Heavens and Earth, the creator of the Universe. He is the Lord of all lords, King of all kings.

He is the Most Compassionate and Most Merciful. Allah Neither Begets, nor is He Begotten. And He knows no equal. God offers a description of Himself in His book, the Holy Quran, stating:

Say, "He is Allah, [who is] One, Allah, the Eternal Refuge. He neither begets nor is born, nor is there to Him any equivalent" (Quran 112:1-4)

The word Allah translates to God. Allah is not a foreign God and does not bear a foreign name. Allah, rather, is the semantic term for God. Regardless of this, some people harbor the mistaken belief that Muslims worship a different God than Christians and Jews; and that 'Allah' is the 'God of the Arabs or God of the Muslims'. This is far from the truth.

The word "Allah" is the Arabic name that connotes the Almighty God. Arabic-speaking Jews and Christians use this same word to refer to God. If one were to peruse an Arabic translation of the Bible, one would see the word 'Allah' being used in place of the term 'God.' However, Muslims, Christians, and Jews all have different concepts of God.

Muslims and Jews both reject the Christian beliefs of the Trinity and the Divine incarnation. This, however, does not mean that each of these three religions worships a different God. There is only One true God.

Muslims prefer to use the name 'Allah' as opposed to the English word 'God' because the English word 'God' can be made plural and can be rendered masculine or feminine; whereas the Arabic word 'Allah' cannot be made plural and is genderless. For instance, if you add the letter 's' to the word God, it becomes 'gods'--which is the plural of God.

In the case of the Arabic word 'Allah,' one cannot make the word plural by adding 's' or in any other way morphing the word's structure. Likewise, if one adds 'ess' to the end of the word 'God,' it becomes 'goddess,' which connotates a female god. God is not female nor male. He is genderless. The word 'Allah' in the Arabic language does not have a gender. It cannot be made feminine.

Muslims reject the use of the word 'God' because it has different connotations to different people. God means different things to different people because the term 'God' indicates an entity worthy of worship; and regretfully, people assign a godlike status to many other beings, divine or otherwise. However, sometimes while speaking to non-Muslims, one may use the word 'God' instead of 'Allah' to help the intended audience understand the context of the word; to relate the message you are referring to the One Supreme Being.

The word Allah comes from the origin of the word *Al-ilah*, which enjoins the two terms 'The' and 'God' as in 'The God.' The term *illah*, which is the closest synonym to God in the Arabic language, is rich and has several meanings. *Illah* refers to an entity worthy of worship and service, an object of devotion and love, someone you turn to in desperate times, someone you adore and think about all the time. *Illah* also is one you turn to for protection, help or aid. You find sanctuary and rest in your *Illah*, who is always present to comfort and guide beings of His creation.

The relationship with God is expressed in the Arabic word *Al-Rabb*, which is used frequently in the Quran. Linguistically it is defined as *'sticking close to something.'* It also means *'joining something with another.'* In the Holy Qur'an, the word *Al-Rabb* implies that the owner (God) has full authority over his property (his servants) and is a Master who ultimately sustains His creation by regulating affairs, providing provisions, and granting all varieties of favors and blessings. *Al-Rabb* also means the One who sustains and nurtures the hearts and souls of His creation.

Muslims believe in One, unique, incomparable God, who has no son, no daughter, no father, no mother, no family, and no partner. He is the Knower of the unseen and the Source of All Mercy. He is the Creator, the Maker, the Fashioner, the Wise. All that is in the Heavens and Earth magnify Him. Muslims believe that none should be worshipped but Him alone. He is the true God, and every other deity is false. None carries the right to be worshipped, revered, adored, invoked, supplicated, or shown any act of worship, but Allah alone.

God is unique, indivisible and similar to nothing. Whenever you try to compare God to anything in this world, it cannot be God; because God, to put it is incomparable. Our finite human minds can fully comprehend and grasp God as a concept. Muslims avoid conceptualizing His image, because imagining or visualizing Him would limit Him. The human imagination is limited, as it is based on what it observes and experiences directly. The human imagination cannot fully grasp the state of God, who is timeless and eternal with no beginning or end. God has a unique nature and is free from gender and human weakness and is beyond anything which human beings can imagine. God states:

"There is no god but He, the Creator of all things; then worship Him, and He has the power to dispose of all affairs. No vision can grasp Him, but His grasp is over all vision; He is the Sublime, Well-Aware"
(Quran 6: 102-103)

God is the King, the Holy, the one free from all defects. The Protector, the Keeper, the Sustainer of Earth and the Universe and all it contains. He is the Glorious, the Great, the Deserving of all Praise. The Kingdom of the Heavens and the Earth belong to Him. Nothing is hidden from Him, and Nothing is beyond His capabilities. He is the Lord and Master of the physical Universe and the Ruler and Lawgiver for human life. Allah is the creator of everything from the smallest to the biggest of things. It is He who heats and brightens the Earth, varies the direction of the winds, and keeps planets in their separate orbits. He is the one that merges the night into the day and merges the day into the night. He is the Master of the Day of Judgement. Allah does not sleep nor slumber, nor sleeps overtake Him. Afterall, created the universe in six days with no rest. God states:

"[He is] Creator of the Heavens and the Earth. He has made for you from yourselves, mates, and among the cattle, mates; He multiplies you thereby. There is nothing like unto Him, and He is the Hearing, the Seeing (Quran 42:11)

God is Loving, Compassionate, Merciful; He is the answerer of prayers, and He is indeed involved and concerned with the daily affairs of all human beings. God is the Beneficent, the Merciful. He is the Giver of life and the Causer of death. He is the Master of the Day of Judgment. He is the Most-High, the most Supreme. He is the most generous and the most loving to his creation. God gives, without measure, to His servants. He gifted mankind life and the ability to hear, feel, taste, and see. God gifted humans their hearts, minds, souls, strengths, and skills.

"And He gave you from all you asked of Him. And if you should count the favor of Allah, you could not enumerate them. Indeed, mankind is [generally] most unjust and ungrateful" (Quran 14:34)

God created all things from nothing. He is in no need of His creation, although His creation is all in need of Him. He is all Knowledgeable and encompasses all things, the open and the secret, the public and the private. He knows all secrets that lay hidden in the hearts and minds of men. He knows of all that happened in the past, what is happening now, and what will happen. Our Lord neither errs nor forgets. He is free from all defects and imperfections. He is the One that accepts repentance from His servants and forgives all sins. Allah knows of what you endure and understands your feelings and struggles. Allah understands because He was there with you all along.

Allah has power over all things. No other power nor might nor strength nor influence can cause benefit or harm to anyone or anything, except that which flows through Him. Nothing can ever happen unless God wills it to be so.

"Not a leaf falls but that He knows it. And no grain is there within the darknesses of the earth and no moist or dry [thing] but that is [written] in a clear record" (Quran 6:59)

God can make anything happen. He states in His book:

"Whenever We will anything to be, We say unto it Our word "Be," and it is" (Quran 16:40)

Some people assume that God, as perceived in the faith of Islam is a harsh, stern, cruel God; one who demands to be respected, worshipped, and obeyed fully, and is not loving and kind to His creation. Nothing could be further from the truth. God is All-Loving. He claims among His names Al-Wadoud in Arabic (the All-Loving). The love of God in the Holy Qur'an is expressed and emphasized many times throughout His Book. God bespeaks His love for the righteous, the charitable, the steadfast, the doers of good, the just, the fair, the benevolent, those who trust Him; the ones that are clean, the ones that purify themselves, and the ones who fulfill their obligations. The entire Universe and everything it contain is proof of Allah's love for all of His creation. He loves us so much that He gave us an endless variety of foods, a vast array of land and wildlife, the sun, the moon, the stars, family, offspring, and much more. Everything one sees feels, hears, tastes, and smells are all forms of blessings, given to us by our Loving Creator. He didn't have to do this, but He bestowed these blessings upon us. His boundless mercy encompasses everything.

"And if you should count the favors of Allah, you could not enumerate them. Indeed, Allah is Forgiving and Merciful" (Quran 16:18)

God is also All-Just. Hence, evildoers and sinners must be held accountable for their actions. God is Holy, Righteous, and Fair. If He didn't punish for evil, He would allow that evil to exist without consequences. Since God cannot let that happen, His justice requires that a proper punishment is incurred and executed for evil sins. Although Allah is not answerable to anyone, He has promised to be Just and Fair to everyone.

He has prohibited injustice against the innocent. Allah never would punish an innocent person, nor hold anyone accountable for the sins of another. Unlike Christianity, Islam imposes no burden of the original sin. Every human being is born with a clean slate and is rewarded or punished only based on one's willful intent, words, and deeds. Allah is the Absolute Judge, the Legislator. God is the One who distinguishes right from wrong. God even is more merciful to His creation than a mother is to her child. God is far removed from injustice and tyranny. He is All-Wise in all of His actions and decrees.

For one to be genuinely devoted to Allah and to love Him above all else imaginable, one needs to have knowledge of God that goes beyond the basic aspects of His role as the sole Creator and Sustainer. To reward any seeker who strives to learn more about the Creator, Allah has revealed a great deal of information about Himself and His Attributes. Allah has the most Magnificent, Beautiful of names and sublime Perfect attributes. No one shares His Divinity, nor His Attributes. Allah's Attributes are incomparable, Greater and more perfectly than those acquired by people, as there is nothing like Him, His Attributes, and Actions.

God has an infinite number of names and has a particular and special category of 99 names listed in the Holy Koran and teachings of the Prophet Muhammad. Of His names is The Ever-Merciful, The Forgiving, The Loving, The Nourisher, The Sustainer, The Compassionate, The Exalter, The Just, The Great, The Protector, The Caregiver, The Ever-Living, The Powerful, The First, The Last, The Pardoner, The Light, The Supporter, The Eternal, The Preserver, The Wise, The Originator, and The One Who Gives Life and Resurrects. If our Creator is Eternal and Everlasting, then His attributes must adhere to this same edict. God has perfect attributes. He has limitless and infinite hearing, vision, mercy, and—above all—love. Muslims attribute certain factors to every quality of God:

None of His attributes ever knew a beginning, nor will they ever have an ending. For instance, He always has been All-Hearing and always will be All-Hearing. Allah hears everything from our inner thoughts and tiniest whispers to the buzz of a mosquito's wing and the eruption of Volcanos. Language is no barrier for Him, for God understands all.

All of His attributes are infinite. Whereas humans can hear only what's in front of them, God can listen to simultaneous conversations inside and outside a room; God can hear all.

All of our attributes as humans were given to us as gifts, whereas all of God's attributes originated within Him. His attributes were not given to Him; they were within Him all along.

The most significant and most honorable knowledge is that of Allah's Names, Attributes, and Actions. God encourages His creation to learn His names so they can discover more about Him. How would one love, worship, fear, and trust God if they do not know His Identity and His Attributes? By learning Allah's names and attributes, one can appreciate His Power over all things and increase the pleasure and sublime awe he or she finds in God's company. That is why knowledge of Allah is a central tenant of the Islamic faith.

It is when one genuinely ponders on the Majesty of Allah, that one's humility increases. Muslims are advised to study and ponder His Names and Attributes and are encouraged to worship and call Him by those names. God states:

"And to Allah belong the best names, so invoke Him by them" (Quran 7:180)

God is above His creation, above the heavens, above His Throne. However, He never is contained by any sort of physical dimension. Allah is close, very close. God is close to those who believe in Him, and He answers their every call. Saying that God is with His servants, does not mean that He intermingles or dwells with His creation; rather He establishes His presence with His creation by His Knowledge and Power. Nothing is hidden from Him of what His creation does or says. God states in the Quran:

"Verily Allah knows all the hidden things of the Heavens and the Earth; Verily He has full Knowledge of all that is in (men's) hearts" (Quran 35:38)

God is very near. He sees and knows every aspect of His creations. He hears every word that is uttered. He is knowledgeable of even one's inner thoughts. God knows all of our dreams, secrets, desires, and wishes. Nothing is hidden from Him.

"We created man, and We know what his own self whispers to him. We are nearer to him than his jugular vein" (Quran 50:36)

Allah is in no need of His creation, although His creation needs Him. Allah wants humans to worship Him for their own benefit. Mankind needs God in their lives at all times and for all purposes. Those who recognize the Majesty of the Creator of All, soon become awestruck and humble in their knowledge. One that rejects God and His Guidance is like a patient refusing a doctor's medicine for his pain. This patient would be foolish, ignorant, and illogical in his actions; as would be one who rejects Allah. Allah is Fully Omnipotent and Self-sufficient. He is in no need of humanistic worship or anything else.

Allah is Perfect

HOLY QURAN

The faith of Islam states that God revealed His Wisdom, Laws, and Instructions through his final Book, the Holy Quran. The Holy Quran says that in every age, a book is revealed. God has sent forth a number of books in the past; but the last and final revelation is the Glorious Quran, which was revealed to the latest and final Prophet, Muhammad peace be upon him.

All Revelations preceding the Holy Quran were sent only to a particular group of people and pertained to a specific period. The final and ultimate revelation, the Holy Qur'an, was not revealed for only a particular group of people—such as Muslims or Arabs—but for all of humanity, until the end of time. A Book of guidance intended not only for the people of his era but for all generations to come until the Last Day.

The Holy Qur'an, sometimes spelled Koran, is the verbatim word of God. Logically, the book embodies and represents God's wishes to send a Message to all of humanity; one meant to be followed till the Day of Judgement and shielded from any changes, subtractions or additions.
Unlike other sacred scriptures like the Bible, the Quran has been perfectly preserved in both its words and meaning—and in a language that still exists today. Whereas Muslims believe that the original Gospel was sent from God to Prophet Jesus peace be upon him for the Israelites, Muslims, and Biblical scholars acknowledge that the Bible was not written by God or Jesus himself; instead written by individuals who lived after the departure of Jesus peace be upon him. Christian Scholars recognize that the Bible has been altered, distorted, and changed during the last centuries so it contains words of man and not the Divine Being. Since human hands altered the previous Scriptures,

the Bible Gospel and the Torah of today, as they are published, do not comprise their exact original scriptures in their pure and unfettered form. God, the Almighty warns in the Holy Koran:

"So woe to those who write the 'scripture' with their own hands, then say, 'This is from Allah,' to exchange it for a small price. Woe to them for what their hands have written and woe to them for what they earn"
(Quran 2:79)

Christian sects do not agree on what exactly qualifies as an 'inspired book' of God. The Protestants are taught that 66 truly inspired books make up the Bible, whereas the Catholics have been taught about the existence of 73 truly 'inspired books.' The first Christians for many generations followed neither the 66 books of the Protestants nor the 73 books of the Catholics.

Whereas the Holy Quran confirms the existence of the Scriptures that were sent before it, including the Jewish Torah and the Gospels of Jesus peace be upon him. The Holy Qur'an abrogates all previous scriptures and becomes the Book of guidance for all humankind.

The Quran was revealed to guide humanity through every aspect of their lives. The Quran is a guide, an instructional manual on how one's life should be lived. The Quran is a personal guide that will navigate one throughout his or her daily struggles. Just as, when you buy a computer or any electronic device, it comes with an instructional manual dictating how the machine should be operated. One is advised to read the instructional manual of life, The Holy Quran, and live in how our Creator has decreed. How would man know his role and the purpose of his existence, unless he receives clear and practical instructions regarding what God wants from him? If one follows the guidelines carefully, then he shall be rewarded with a better life; here in this world, and the Hereafter. If you disobey God and go against His commands, then you will face the consequences in this world and the hereafter.

The Quran is the primary source of Islam for all Muslims. The Book is and always has been written in the Arabic language. The Quran is so unique in content and style that it cannot be translated; therefore, any translation is to be taken only as an interpretation of the meanings of the Quran.

Distinctions must be drawn between the Holy Quran and its translations. Any translations of the Quran are not the Quran in its true and pure form; it is merely a translation and explanation of the Original Masterwork authored by the Almighty. A translation of the Koran is not the word of God. Different translations of the Quran are intended to help non-Arabic speaking audiences comprehend its meaning; still and all, there is only One Quran. Since each translation of the Quran is not the original work and is only human-made in content, it is an imperfect translation bound to contain errors. Some translations may be superior to others in their linguistic style or their interpretations of the Quran. There remains Only One true version of this timeless Book as only the original Quran contains the exact Arabic words spoken by God; revealed to Prophet Muhammad peace be upon him by the Angel Gabriel

If a Muslim in Asia reads a verse of the Koran, one can be sure another Muslim is reciting the same words in faraway Africa. No differences will exist between the two reciting. God has promised always to preserve the Quran, protecting His Book from anyone attempts to modify or change its Text or Message. This means that God will guard His Book against any human-made modifications, distortions, additions, subtractions, or tampering in any form. God states in the Quran:

"Indeed, it is We who sent down the Qur'an, and indeed, We will be its Guardian"   (Quran 15:9)

The word 'Quran' linguistically translates to 'recitation,' meaning the recitation of the words of God the Glorious via the Angel Gabriel to Prophet Muhammad. Then the Prophet peace be upon him recited these same words to the people. As mentioned earlier, Muslims also believe in the Gospel and the Torah; but the Holy Quran is the final Testament of God, the complete word of God, supplying Guidance for all people living now and going forward.

The Quran first was revealed in the Holy Month of Ramadan — which is the 9th month of the Islamic Lunar Calendar. The remainder of its Message was revealed bit by bit for the next 23 years. Each passage was revealed in the wake of a significant event in the life of the Prophet Muhammad peace be upon him. Finally, it was then put together as a whole in his lifetime.

The Quran is a widely known and memorized Document. The Quran is the only book that is memorized by millions of people of all ages around the world, of all languages and backgrounds, from one end to the other. The Quran is the most widely and frequently read Book in the world, both today and over the last millennium. Even without the benefit of a photographic memory, children and adults in Asia, Africa, Europe, and across the globe, have memorized this Book which contains over 600 pages word for word. Almost every Muslim has memorized some portion of the Holy Quran to read in his/her prayers. This is due to Allah's kept promise regarding the Quran's content it was created and designed to be easy to understand and memorize.

"And in truth, We have made the Quran easy to remember; who, then, is willing to take it to heart?" (Quran 54:17)

Prophet Muhammad peace be upon him was commanded by God to convey the contents of the Holy Quran to the people. This was a tremendous responsibility that weighed heavily upon him.

"And We have not revealed to you the Book, [O Muhammad], except for you to make clear to them that wherein they have differed and as guidance and mercy for a people who believe" (Quran 16:64)

The Quran deals with all subjects which concern human beings, such as doctrine, wisdom, worship, law, transactions, and more. Its central theme is the relationship between God and His creation. The Quran teaches the art of living. The Quran contains guidelines and teachings, for both individuals and society. The Quran also provides guidelines and instructions for proper human conduct, a fair economic system, ritual worship, ethics and moral behavior, business, government, and more.

The Quran contains signs of God's Greatness: miracles, parables, and lessons. The Quran explains the concept of God, His Names, and Attributes. It details what is permissible and what is forbidden; it teaches the basics of good manners and morals and contains rulings and guidelines about how to worship God and live. The Quran also describes the appearance and characteristics of Paradise and Hell. The Quran tells stories of past nations and their mistakes, not to incite hate but to teach lessons that will educate us against making the same mistakes they did. The purpose and aim of these stories are that we learn from the excellent role models and bad examples found in our past. The Quran calls upon humanity to believe in God, His angels, His Books, His Messengers, the Last Day, in fate and the divine decree.

The Quran is like no other book, because it serves as an infinite source of intellectual wisdom and spiritual elevation. It cleanses the heart. The Holy Quran teaches that one should be truthful and never to lie or cheat. The Quran teaches us to give charity to the poor and to be kind to our parents, neighbors, family, and friends.

Despite what you may have heard of the Quran, the Holy Book does not teach hate, violence, or killing. The Quran is a book based on love, compassion, faith, and goodwill. The Quran calls it:

"...The ways of peace" (Quran 5:16)

and describes:

"...reconciliation as the best policy" (Quran 4:128)

The Quran states that:

"...God abhors any disturbance of peace" (Quran 2:205)

There are many verses throughout the Quran the demonstrate God's love for peace and good, and he commands humanity to:

"Speak kindly" (Quran 2:83)
"Speak Politely" (Quran 17:53)
"Speak Justice" (Quran 6:152)
"Speak the truth" (Quran 3:17)
"Speak no lie" (Quran 22:30)
"Speak not in vain" (Quran 22:30)
"Speak graciously" (Quran 17:23)
"Speak fairly" (Quran 17:28)

God reminds us of His love, compassion, and mercy in introducing 113 out of his 114 chapters in His Holy Book with the statement, *'In the name of God, the Most Gracious/Loving, the most Merciful.'* If you go through the pages of the Quran, you will see endless examples of God's love, mercy, compassion, forgiveness, and justice for all of his creations. The Quran is also a Book of hope. God reminds humankind not to give in to despair. No matter what sins one may have committed, those who turn to God with regret seeking forgiveness will be forgiven, and his salvation assured.

Contrary to popular belief, the Quran forces no one to turn to Islam against their will. It compels no one to live by Islamic morals. While the conveying and teaching of God and the morals of the Qur'an to others is a duty of Muslims, they call people to the path of God only with kindness and love and never force them to anything. God states in His book:

"There shall be no compulsion in [acceptance of] the religion. The right course has become clear from the wrong. So, whoever disbelieves in false deities and believes in Allah has grasped the most trustworthy handhold with no break in it, And Allah is Hearing and Knowing"
(Quran 2:256)

The values of the Qur'an hold a Muslim responsible for treating all people, whether or not Muslim, fairly, kindly and justly. The Quran teaches the importance of protecting and taking care of the needy, the orphans, and the innocent. The Quran prevents and warns about the spreading of mischief, unlawful killing, fraud, envy, intoxicants, and the mistreatment of humans, animals, and plants. God states:

"And when he goes away, he strives throughout the land to cause corruption therein and destroy crops and animals. And Allah does not like corruption" (Quran 2:205)

Islam has two primary sources, the Holy Quran and the authentic traditions/sayings of the final Prophet, Muhammad peace be upon him, which explain and sometimes expand upon the concepts presented in the Quran.

The Quran is meant to be read aloud and in a reverent and melodious tone. The Quran is composed of 114 units or chapters, called a surah in Arabic, and each sentence or phrase of the Quran is called an 'Aaya,' which translates to mean a 'Sign'; as it is a sign that God exists. The word 'Aaya' also has the associative meanings of 'miracles' or 'proof,' that describes the Verses in the Quran. The Quran was not meant to tell a chronological story, and thus should not be viewed as a sequential narrative like the Book of Genesis.

Prophet Muhammad peace be upon him did not author this Book. The Quran was sent down to a Prophet that was unlettered, that did not read, write or calculate, and that had no education; these characteristics serving as sufficient proof he did not author the Holy Text. The Quran challenges anyone who doubts the Book's Divine origins to produce another sacred text equal in merit. Any document that claims to include the word of God bears a heavy burden. Without clear evidence or with the presence of one contradiction found within the Book, the apparent word of God would be proven false. The Quran is devoid of contradictions, nor does it contain any information confirmed to be false.

The Quran is a living miracle of the Arabic language; it is inimitable in its style, form and spiritual impact. The Quran is miraculous because it achieves linguistic perfection in the Arabic language. For instance, the Quran explains complicated legal matters like inheritance with the use of simple speech and imagery in the Arabic language. The Quran has its unique rhythm, style, rhyme, and genre, and is like no other book. The fact that the Quran uses futuristic terminology and descriptions, reaching far beyond the knowledge and comprehension of a 7th-century person living in the desert, is a miracle.

The Quran is a miracle as it contains hundreds of scientific facts later confirmed to be accurate, years after the book was revealed. The Quran is a miracle because of the power and effect it wields for human beings all over the world. It changes millions of people's lives and views. It transforms people into better human beings. The Quran is a miracle because of its incredible spiritual power and psychological effects. The Quran is a miracle because of how it changed and impacted human history in so many ways throughout the years.

Whereas the Quran contains accounts of hundreds of scientific miracles, the Quran is not a book of science--nor is it a book of engineering or medicine. The Quran is a book of guidance and signs that prove its divinity. As the faith of Islam continued to grow century after century, we evolved into the age of modern science. In this era, many scientific discoveries began to confirm many related verses of the Quran.

The Quran is the greatest miracle of God. The Quran is proof of the truthfulness of Islam. The Quran is the standing and ever-lasting wonder and miracle. The Quran is such a significant miracle that all others are considered trivial compared to the Quran. The Quran is a document that contains thousands of miracles to prove its Godly origins. It includes accounts of miracles as they occur and expand from one dimension to another.

MESSENGERS &
PROPHETS OF GOD

How would one know the role and life purpose of existence unless one receives clear and practical instructions of what God wants and expects of him or her? Here comes the need for Prophethood. Thus, God has sent thousands of Prophets and Messengers to humankind. Every nation on Earth received a Prophet. God states in the Quran:

"And We certainly sent into every nation a messenger, [saying], "Worship Allah and shun False Gods, and among them were those whom Allah guided, and among them were those upon whom error was [deservedly] decreed. So, proceed through the Earth and observe how was the end of the deniers" (16:36)

They all preached the same general message that there is only one deity worthy of worship. He is the One and Only God, without a partner, son, daughter, or equal. All other gods are false and are only creations of God and not the actual Creator. All the Prophets and Messengers came with the same purpose, to lead humanity to God. Muslims believe that God communicates His guidance through human Prophets. Belief in the prophets who God relayed His Message to humanity is a required article of the Islamic faith. God states:

"The Prophet (Muhammad) believes in what has been sent down to him from his Lord, and (so do) the believers. Each one believes in God, His Angels, His Books, and His prophets. (They say,) 'We make no distinction between one another of His prophets...'' (Quran 2:285)

The Prophets seek nothing for their personal interest in this world. Instead, they seek things for the public interest by warning their people against what may harm them. God sent Prophets to humanity for several reasons, for instance, to guide humanity from worshipping created beings and to worship their Creator, the Creator of all things. The Prophets came to guide humankind to build a relationship with their Creator, to know Him and to love Him. The Prophets taught humanity that life is only a test where the successful will enter Heaven eternally, and the unsuccessful will enter the hellfire. Prophets and Messengers were sent to teach humanity about righteousness, morals, ethics, and how to purify their souls from evil.

They were also sent to teach about the unseen world which exists beyond our ordinary senses and physical universe, such as the existence of the Angels. God sent Prophets and Messengers to stand as witnesses on the Day of Judgement to the ones that will claim they never heard the message.

Muslims believe, respect, honor, and love all Prophets and Messengers of God, starting with Prophet Adam, including Noah, Abraham, Ishmael, Jacob, Moses, and Prophet Jesus peace be upon them all, all who invited people to worship God and shun false gods. Muslims believe in many of the Prophets found in Jewish and Christian traditions.

Muslims also believe in God's final Testament to man, which was revealed to the last and final Prophet; Prophet Muhammad peace be upon him, who was sent to the last and final nation, our nation. God states in the Quran:

"Muhammad is not the father of any one of your men, but he is the Messenger of God and the last of the prophets" (Quran 33:40)

Out of the Infinite Mercy and Love of God, God continued to send Prophets and Revelations to guide humanity. Each Prophet and Book was sent down to different nations and people. There were over one hundred thousand Prophets and Messengers sent to all of humanity, to all nations and races, in all corners of the world. Some Prophets were superior to others. The best among them were Prophets Noah, Abraham, Moses, Jesus, and Prophet Muhammad peace be upon them. God states:

Islam states, all the previous Prophets and Books other than the Holy Quran and Prophet Muhammad were sent down only for a particular nation and a specific group of people and were only meant to be followed for a particular period. For example, Muslims believe Prophet Jesus peace be upon him was one of God's mightiest messengers of God who was sent down with the same general Message of all the previous Prophets but was only sent to the Children of Israel as their final Prophet because they were veering away from the laws and disobeying the commandments of God. Prophet Jesus' mission was to confirm the Torah that was previously sent, to make certain lawful things that were previously unlawful to ease their lives and to proclaim and re-affirm the belief in One God. Prophet Jesus peace be upon him was not meant for the non-Israelites.

God states in his final Revelation in the Holy Quran that He would teach Prophet Jesus peace be upon him the Torah, the Gospel, and the Wisdom.

"And He will teach him writing and Wisdom and the Torah and the Gospel" (Quran 3:48)

To spread his message to the Israelites, Prophet Jesus peace be upon him was taught the Torah, and he was provided with his own Revelation from God, the Gospel (Injeel). God also bestowed Prophet Jesus peace be upon him with the ability to guide and influence his people with signs and miracles to prove he was sent down by God. The miracles were proof he wasn't an imposter. All the wonders and miracles that were granted by Prophet Jesus or any Prophet of God is only done with the permission and power of God and are usually in the field in which his people excel and are recognized as superior at the time and place of the Prophet.

People of later generations disoriented all the earlier Revelations of God. As a result, pure Revelation from God was polluted with myths, words of men, superstitions, irrational philosophical ideologies, and idol worship. The religion of God was lost in a plethora of religions.

Later, when humanity was in the depth of dark ages, God the Almighty sent his last and final Messenger Prophet Muhamad and his final Revelation, the Holy Koran, to redeem humanity. The Koran and the final Messenger peace be upon him affirmed everything that was revealed to all the previous messengers in the past.

Since past Revelations were meant for past nations, The Holy Qur'an and the way of Prophet Muhammad abrogates all the previous laws. By the Wisdom of God, He did not allow the teachings of the earlier prophets to remain preserved in an entirely undistorted manner. There will be no Prophet, or Book after The Holy Koran and Prophet Mohamad peace be upon him. Prophet Mohamad was not only sent down to the Arabs or Muslims, rather was sent down for all of humanity till the end of time. The Quran states:

"And We have not sent you (O Muhammad) except as a bringer of glad tidings and a warner unto all humanity, but most people know not" (Quran 34:28)

God chose the best among humanity to deliver His Message. Prophethood is not earned or acquired thru certain practices or higher education. God chooses whom He pleases and thinks would be the best fit for this purpose. The Prophets and Messengers were best in morals and manners and were mentally and physically fit for the task and were protected by God from falling into major sins. The Prophets were the best in their community morally and intellectually so they can serve as good role models for their followers. Their personality was one that attracted people to accept their Message rather than drive people away. They did not err nor commit mistakes in delivering the Message. All of God's messengers preached the same general Message. They preached there is Only One God; one should love Him with All his heart, Worship Him to his or her best ability & praise Him and Follow His Laws.

The Prophet's Messages came with glad tidings and a warning. The glad tidings were for those who believe informing them that their past sins will be forgiven, and a generous reward of Paradise will be awarded to them. The warning is for those who disbelieve informing them that if they continue their evil ways, their final destination will be the hellfire. The Quran states:

"Verily! We have sent you with the truth, a bearer of glad tidings, and a warner. And there never was a nation, but a warner had passed among them" (Quran 35:24)

and the Quran also states:

"Verily, those who fear their Lord unseen, theirs will be forgiveness and a great reward" (Quran 67:12)

Prophet Muhammed was sent with a Message in the language of the people he was sent upon. So, they can easily understand the Message, apply it in their lives, and then convey it to others. If he had not carried the Message in their language, they would not have understood him. Since Prophet Muhammad was sent to the Arabs speaking plain Arabic, they had no excuse but to hear his message. God states in the Quran:

"And We never punish until We have sent a Messenger (to give warning)" (Quran 17:15)

Prophet Muhamad's Message was certainly not limited to the people of his time. Instead, Prophet Muhammad was sent to all of humanity. This is stated repeatedly in the Qur'an. Whereas Prophet Muhammad was an Arab, only 4 of the 25 mentioned Prophets in the Holy Qur'an were Arabs. The Arab Prophets were Prophet Hud (Eber in English), Prophet Saleh, Prophet Shuaib (known in the Biblical literature as Jethro) and Prophet Muhammad peace be upon them. Prophet Muhammad is only mentioned four times in the Koran by name. The most mentioned Prophet in the Quran is Moses. Prophet Moses peace be upon him is mentioned in over 70 passages.

Prophet Moses was the most mentioned Prophet in the Quran because he was the most similar to Prophet Muhammad and his nation was the most similar to our nation so we could learn and benefit from their mistakes. In reading and learning what happened to the Israelites and their errors, our nation can avoid making the same mistakes they made. One-way God delivers his guidance to humanity is through giving examples of past nations, their stories, and their mistakes, so people now can benefit, not make the same mistakes, and live their lives accordingly. The Almighty states:

"There was certainly in their stories a lesson for those of understanding. Never was the Qur'an a narration invented, but a confirmation of what was before it and a detailed explanation of all

things and guidance and mercy for a people who believe" (Quran 12:111)

In each story mentioned in the Quran, there are many lessons. People went to extremes with the Prophets that were sent from God. Some Prophets were rejected and accused of being sorcerers, madmen, Forgers, Plagiarizers, Magicians, Poets, soothsayers, imposters, and liars, even though they came with miracles and Books beyond the power of humans, to prove they were sent from God. For instance, Prophet Jesus peace be upon him, son of Mary, was rejected by the Jews and they refused to consider him to be the Messenger they had been waiting for. The Jews rejected Prophet Jesus and Prophet Muhamad, even though their Book spoke about an upcoming Prophet that will come *'I will establish a Prophet for them from among their brothers, like you, and I will place My words in his mouth; and he shall speak to them all that I shall command him'* (Devarim 18:18). This Prophet was no other than the Prophet Muhamad peace be upon him.

The Christians also rejected Prophet Muhamad. However, Muslims believe in all Prophets sent from God starting with Prophet Adam to the last and final Prophet, Prophet Muhamad. Muslims accept all Prophets and Messengers of God who brought guidance to humanity. However, the Revelations which the Prophets before Prophet Muhammad brought from God have been tampered with by men over the years. Since the Bible was sent down for a particular group of people and a particular period, God did not feel it fit to preserve the Bible. It is now mixed with words of men and contains hundreds of scientific errors which prove it's no longer in the same form as it once was when Prophet Jesus peace be upon him was present.

Since the Holy Quran is meant for all of humanity as a whole and is intended to eternity. God made sure he preserved it from being tampered with. The Quran is the only Book of God that remains untampered, untouched, whole, standing the same form as it came down over 1400 years ago. God states in the Quran:

"Indeed, it is We who sent down the Qur'an, and indeed, We will be its guardian (guard it against corruption)" (Quran 15:9)

While some took the Prophets as a joke and rejected them, some, on the contrary, turned Prophets into gods by giving them divine powers or declared them to be children of God like with Prophet Jesus with the Christians. Prophets are to be loved and respected, but no form of worship is to be directed towards them nor are they to be treated as demi-gods or intermediaries between mankind and God. However, Christians appointed him to divine heights that he was not entitled to. Jesus' Message lasted in its original purity for some time. While the Israelites and the Roman authorities rejected his Message, there were a group of people that accepted and believed in his Message called his disciples. Soon after God elevated Prophets Jesus soul and body to Heaven.

The early devoted followers of Jesus tried to maintain the purity and clarity of his teachings; that he is only a Messenger of God. Jesus' Message lasted in its original purity for some time, but the Scripture he received was slowly altered and his original Message of the absolute Oneness of God. Soon later, in the next few centuries, different beliefs about Prophet Jesus developed amongst some early Christians. They claimed that he was divine, calling him the son of God, which eventually became the dominant Christian belief.

Six centuries after Jesus, God sent His last and final Messenger Muhammad to mankind with His final scripture, known as the Holy Quran. If Jesus claimed to be God then there would be many verses in the Bible which would have mentioned so, however, there is not a single verse in the entire Bible that states Jesus said 'I am God' or 'worship me' Furthermore the Bible itself calls Jesus a Prophet: *"When Jesus entered Jerusalem, the whole city was stirred and asked, Who is this? The crowds answered. This is Jesus, the Prophet from Nazareth in Galilee"* (*Matthew 21:10-11*). How could Prophet Jesus be God and God's Prophet at the same time? That wouldn't make any logical sense. Jesus never claimed he was God, or he should be worshipped. Jesus never claimed divinity. All Prophets and Messengers were created human beings who had no divine attributes, power or any divine qualities of God. They were the best slaves of God that walked the Earth; who ate, drank, slept, and lived normal human lives.

PAST NATIONS

All of God's Prophets came with miracles (signs of God's existence) to prove God sent them. Islam defines a miracle as an extraordinary act or event that go against the laws of nature and can only come about through the direct intervention and will of God. Miracles are not magic, which by definition are only tricks or illusions. Acts of Magic are evil acts performed with the help of devils. Prophets can only achieve miracles. They supported past Prophets as irrefutable evidence proving that their Prophethood was, in fact, a matter of truth. The Prophets were supported by miracles that their nations excelled in so the acts would be more convincing, understood, appreciated and identified by the people of that nation and not thought of just magic.

For instance, the people of Egypt excelled in magic and sorcery and felt they had reached the pinnacle of these evil acts as they often were in contact with Jinn (spirits) to play illusions on people. Thus, God provided Prophet Moses peace be upon him types of miracles that were related to illusions, such as the power to transform his staff into a snake right before his people. He was also able to strike the Nile with his rod to transform the river into blood and part the Red Sea. All meant to humble his people and remind that the power, control, and might of God is true and not just an illusion of the eyes.

Likewise, during the time of Prophet Jesus peace be upon him, the Romans pride themselves in their medicine, healing, cures, and best doctors on the land when medical science was at its height. Thus, God sent down Prophet Jesus peace be upon him with several miracles all coming from this nature which could not be justified by medical science. These miracles include the miraculous birth of Prophet Jesus of a virgin. Prophet Jesus could heal individuals with leprosy, cure the blind, and resurrect the dead all with the permission and will of God. The Almighty states:

"[The Day] when Allah will say, "O Jesus, Son of Mary, remember My favor upon you and upon your mother when I supported you with the Pure Spirit, and you spoke to the people in the cradle and maturity; and [remember] when I taught you writing and wisdom and the Torah and the Gospel; and when you designed from clay [what was] like the form of a bird with My permission, then you breathed into it, and it became a bird with My permission; and you healed the blind and the leper with My permission; and when you brought forth the dead with My permission; and when I restrained the Children of Israel from [killing] you when you came to them with clear proofs and those who disbelieved among them said, "This is not but obvious magic" (Quran 5:110)

Past Prophets had miracles one can only see if they lived in that time to witness it. After the Prophets died, their miracles turned in to stories the following generations can only narrate and not witness. For instance, someone that witnessed Prophet Moses peace be upon him transform his staff into a snake or someone that saw Prophet Jesus peace be upon him give life to a dead person with the permission of God can only share it with his children, and his children can narrate it to their children, and so forth. However, for the generations that were not alive or present to witness the miracles, they became only stories to them. All previous miracles were limited to its time and place. However, for our nation, God has provided our Prophet, Muhammad peace be upon him with a miracle, the Holy Quran, to be witnessed by everyone for all the upcoming generations. The miracle is as convincing, persuasive, compelling, and relevant now as it was when it was first revealed 1400+ years ago. The Quran is a miracle for the eyes to see and the ears to hear. Since the Quran is the final Book for humanity, it had to outlive Prophet Muhamad peace be upon him, so it was audible.

In the time of Prophet Muhammad, the Arabs, although predominantly unlettered, were masters of the spoken word. They were people that excelled in the art of eloquence and knowledge. Their poetry and spoken word were considered a model of literary excellence and they valued spoken word and speech. Thus, God revealed to his final nation, the best and the most eloquent of all speeches, the Holy Quran which left the people of Prophet Muhamad peace be upon him, astounded in terms of eloquence and other terms. The Book was revealed to a Prophet who was unlettered, unable to read, write or calculate to prove to the people his Prophet was not the author. Billions of people since the advent of this miracle have witnessed it, believed in it because of its miraculous nature in terms of its style, content and spiritual uplifting.

The Holy Quran mentions recounted stories of previous nations that were sent down Prophets and Messengers to convey God's Message. But the people rejected, disobeyed, and denied the truth. God states:

"And nothing has prevented Us from sending signs except that the former peoples denied them..." (Quran 17:59)

Between Prophet Adam and Prophet Noah peace be upon them were ten centuries. Amongst the people of that period were righteous individuals that obeyed the laws taught by Prophet Adam and worshipped God accordingly. As time passed, people started to veer away from the remembrance of God. Certain righteous men amongst them would remind the people of their obligations to God. Later, the righteous men began to die, and Satan, the enemy of mankind, came whispering to the people who had looked up to these righteous individuals, putting thoughts into their minds in his sly, deceptive ways, inspiring the people to erect statues in their memory to remember to worship God. After these statutes were built across the land, Satan later came back to the people who had forgotten the reason these statues were constructed. Satan then suggested to the people to worship the statues directly. He told them that their forefathers had worshiped these statues. Out of these people's ignorance, idol worship started. Soon after, Allah sent Messengers after Messengers to guide people to the right path. God states in his Book:

"Satan has overcome them and made them forget the remembrance of Allah. Those are the party of Satan. Unquestionably, the party of Satan - they will be the losers" (Quran 58:19)

God sent Prophet Noah peace be upon him to his people where he preached for 950 years, calling people to worship one God and follow his commandments, but only a few people believed in him. His people denied, mocked him and stated that he is nothing special but another human being amongst them. Prophet Noah peace be upon him agreed he was only human, but he was sent from God the Glorious with a clear warning. After the denial. God instructed Noah to build an ark.

"And construct the ship under Our observation and Our inspiration and do not address Me concerning those who have wronged; indeed, they are [to be] drowned" (Quran 11:37)

As he was building the Ark, his people accuse him of being a madman for building a ship made of planks and nails on land, nowhere near any body of water. Soon, water started to gush from the Earth and fall from the sky; God instructed Noah to enter the Ark with the ones that believed in the Message. He also commanded Prophet Noah to take a male and female of every animal aboard. Then God caused a great flood where water gushed from every crack on the Earth, and rain fell from the skies like never before. Prophet Noah peace be upon him saw his son overwhelmed by the water, so he cried out to him, pleading him to board the Ark and to leave the non-believers to their fate. However, his son was thinking in terms of this worldly life and did not rely on the Trust and Word of God. He replied to his dad he would go to a mountain where the waves could not reach. Noah pleaded with his son saying:

"...There is no protector today from the decree of God, except for whom He gives mercy..." (Quran 11:43)

His son refused. God then stated:

"...O Earth, swallow your water, and O sky, withhold [your rain]." And the water subsided, and the matter was accomplished, and the ship came to rest on the [mountain of] Judiyy. And it was said, "Away with the wrongdoing people" (Quran 11:44)

Soon, his son was drowned. He was drowned with the disbelievers and Noah's wife, who also disbelieved. The flood had cleansed the Earth of idol worshippers and disbelievers. Not a single person who had disbelieved in God remained on the Earth. The ship remains intact upon Judi right until today. An archeological study found the 500-foot long boat-shaped formation atop Mount Judi. God left it as a sign for mankind.

Prophet Hud (Eber in English) peace be upon him was sent to an ancient tribe called Ad who is believed to have been positioned in an area of curved sand hills of Oman and Yemen. They worshiped idols as gods which they believed would provide them happiness and wealth and protect them from evil, harm, and all catastrophes. The people of Prophet Hud were very tall, strong, and well built. They were arrogant people who would boast and tyrannize people with their large size. According to the Quran, they would say:

"Who is greater than us in strength?" (Quran 41:15)

They were known to build lofty towers; thus, the area became known as the land of a thousand pillars since God blessed them with fertile soil and abundant agriculture, many children, an ample supply of livestock and easy access to water resources. They mistakenly understood the purpose of life was to accumulate wealth, prestige, and live in luxury. Prophet Hud would command them to fear God and be righteous. According to the Holy Koran, Prophet Hud peace be upon him would say to his people:

"...O my people, worship Allah; you have no deity other than Him. You are not but inventors [of falsehood]" (Quran 11:50)

Their Prophet advised them to seek God's forgiveness for their heedlessness and arrogance and advised them that if they seek forgiveness, God will increase them in power, strength and wealth. According to the Quran, Prophet Hud would state:

"And O my people, ask forgiveness of your Lord and then repent to Him. He will send [rain from] the sky upon you in showers and increase you in strength [added] to your strength. And do not turn away, [being] criminals" (Quran 11:52)

However, they proudly saw themselves as the most powerful nation in existence. They rejected their Prophet's Message believing that after death their bodies would decay to dust and be swept away by the wind. With their hearts and minds filled with the accumulation of this world, they would say to their Prophet: *'Why did God chose you when you do not differ from the rest of us, you eat and drink like the rest of us.'*

Prophet Hud's people proudly stated: *'Have you come to turn us away from our gods? Then bring upon us the calamity with which you threaten us if you are telling the truth!'* Prophet Hud peace be upon him turned to God the Almighty and renounced his people. Soon after, the people of Hud suffered through a three-year famine and a drought which spread throughout the once green, fertile and abundant land. The people looked to the sky hoping to see signs of rain. One fateful day the weather changed. The burning heat changed to furious violent winds which God the Almighty imposed on them, for seven nights and eight days. The winds ripped apart their homes, possessions, clothing and even the skin on their bodies. The sands of their desert swallowed and buried their crops. Only Prophet Hud and his small band of believers were saved and are believed to have migrated to the Hadhramaut area of what is today known as Southern Yemen. God states:

"Have you not considered how your Lord dealt with 'Aad - [With] Iram - who had lofty pillars, The likes of whom had never been created in the land?" (Quran 89:6-8)

God also speaks in the Quran of a nation where he sent one of his Messengers named Saleh peace be upon him. He was sent to a tribe called 'Thamud.' While many of the Prophets mentioned in the Quran are Prophets shared with Christianity and Judaism, thus their stories are mentioned in the Bible, Muslims additionally believe in all the past Messengers and Prophets of God. Prophet Saleh is not mentioned in the Bible today.

Similar to the people of Hud, the people of Prophet Saleh were also people that cultivated rich, prosperous, vibrant, fertile land, led excessive wealthy lives, built grand buildings, and had become vain because of their wealth. Regretfully, with their extravagant lifestyles came the worship of many gods, oppressing of the poor and living of a life which went against their Lord's commandments.

Prophet Saleh was a pious, righteous man who held a position of leadership in their community, but his call to worship God alone angered many of his people. Prophet Saleh's Message was like all the other Prophets; he warned his people to turn away from worshipping false gods and to follow the One God, Allah, who provided them all their substance. He advised them to thank their One True Creator and urged the rich to stop oppressing the poor and to end all mischief and evil in the land.

The people of Thamud gathered in the shadows of a high mountain where they demanded that Prophet Saleh peace be upon him to prove that the One God, he spoke of was truly Mighty and Strong. They asked him to perform a miracle; they challenged him to produce for them an incomparable she-camel out which must be ten months pregnant, tall and attractive which will emerge from the rock. Prophet Saleh asked them if a she-camel appeared would they then believe in his Message. They responded yes and prayed with Prophet Saleh for the miracle to emerge. By the power and will of God, a massive, pregnant she-camel emerged from the rocks at the bottom of the mountain. They saw a powerful, clear sign from their Lord. Several Prophet Salah's people believed, yet most of them continued in their disbelief and stubbornness even though they witness a great miracle. The Quran states:

"And nothing has prevented Us from sending signs except that the former peoples denied them. And We gave Thamud the she-camel as a visible sign, but they wronged her. And We send not the signs except as a warning" (Quran 17:69)

The she-camel lived among people of Thamud. Later, the people began to complain that the camel drank too much water and frightened the other livestock. Prophet Saleh peace be upon him began to fear for the camel. He warned his people of great a suffering that would befall them if they harmed the she-camel.

"And O my people, this is the she-camel of Allah - [she is] to you a sign. So let her feed upon Allah's Earth and do not touch her with harm, or you will be taken by an impending punishment" (Quran 11:64)

A group of his people got together and plotted to kill the she-camel. When they approached her, they shot their arrow and pierced her with a sword. They cheered and congratulated each other while mocking and laughing at their

Prophet. Then they challenged Prophet Saleh to have God punish them for it. Their Prophet warned them that a great punishment would be upon them within three days while hoping his people would realize their mistake and repent for their massive error. Prophet Saleh and the believers then departed together to Palestine to be saved from God's upcoming punishment. Soon, the sky was filled with lightning and thunder, and the Earth shook aggressively with a frightening earthquake or volcanic eruption. No one, including their idols, could save them.

The result of these nation's was destruction. According to the Quran, when punishment came to these sinners, their only last utterance was:

"...Indeed, we were wrongdoers!" (Quran 7:5)

In the end, they cried out for mercy, but it was too late:

"(When they approached their doom) they cried out (for deliverance), but the time for deliverance was already past" (Quran 38:3)

This brings us to an important point, why is there past nations that rejected, hid, denied, and buried the Message of their Prophets and Messengers? There are several reasons for this. The Message that the Prophets came with went against everything these nations were brought up and raised to believe and went against the beliefs of their forefathers. These people had a strong attachment to the customs of their forefathers and were sensitive concerning the good name of their fathers. They took pride in following their footsteps whether right or wrong. They grew up worshipping idols then the Prophets came and told them they were wrong and only Allah Alone is worthy of worship without partners and sons. The polytheists (idol worshippers) felt the Prophets wanted to dethrone their gods and did not tolerate the Muslims' rejection of their gods and reacted with severe harassment and abuse. God states in the Quran:

"And when it is said to them, 'Follow what Allah has revealed,' they say, 'Rather, we will follow that which we found our fathers doing.' Even though their fathers understood nothing, nor were they guided? The example of those who disbelieve is like that of one who shouts at what

hears nothing but calls and cries cattle or sheep - deaf, dumb and blind, so they do not understand" (Quran 2:170-171)

God shares a conversation between Prophet Abraham peace be upon him and the idol worshippers at his time which included his father:

"When he said to his father and his people, 'What do you worship?' They said, 'We worship idols and remain to them devoted.' He said, 'Do they hear you when you supplicate? Or do they benefit you, or do they harm?' They said, 'But we found our fathers doing thus' (Quran 26:70-74)

The disbelievers of some nations rejected their Prophet because they were mere mortals who ate, drank, and walked the markets like everyone else. To be convinced of their Prophethood they arrogantly wanted God to send an Angel down from Heaven to accompany him. Other unbelievers accused their Prophet of incorporating into his alleged Revelation myths, legends, and fables that were well known to the people of that time. God states in His Book:

"Even when they come to you arguing with you, those who disbelieve say, "This is not but legends of the former peoples." (Quran 6:25)

Certain nations believed in many gods, and some of their cities were dedicated to these gods. They allowed people from all around to come and worship their idols. If Islam told them they were wrong, and that Allah is the Only One that should be worshiped, and all other gods are false, their city would decline in visitors and revenue. It would be the end of their political and economic domination. Greed, selfishness, money, and power got the best of them.

The Prophets came to nations with immense difficulties and conditions. This call to true Islam took the slumbering men by surprise. These people's customs and habits were sunk low. Adultery, liquor, gambling, violence, stealing, dishonesty, murder and many illicit practices were widespread among them. These were all condemned by Islam, and embracing Islam meant leaving all of them and adopting a new mode of life, and many were unwilling to change their wicked old habits. In addition, there was the desire for worldly things which had become so predominant in them, they soon became slaves to their desires, that nothing could move them from this, not even the command of God the Almighty. Islam came down to free people from being slaves to their desires and constant needs for material goods that could never make one permanently happy.

A certain number of these nations contained proud and arrogant people that considered no one else his or her equal. Slaves were mainly looked down upon and were wrongfully treated. Soon after, Islam came down and sought to stop the pride and racism and to establish a universal brotherhood. Islam taught people whether one is the slave or the master, they are both in the same level, and the best amongst them were only the ones with the most piety, righteousness, fear and God consciousness. This angered many of the tribe's chieftains.

God, the Almighty has mentioned the stories of perished nations and their wrongdoings in the Holy Quran to warn our nation from making the same mistakes they did. The repeating of the same mistakes they made can lead to the same outcome. Unfortunately, the current average Muslim hardly recites Quran with deep reflection, pondering over its profound Verses and Signs. By comparing the past nations to our nation, one would conclude that our nation is in danger. People today do the same sinful deeds that were done in the past. We see the same errors happening now, that happened in the past, such as disobeying God's commandments and associating partners with Him, behaving arrogantly, wrongfully, and sinfully. All the nations of the past have been punished through natural disasters. God has given our nation warnings that if we repeat the same errors and sins the past nations did, we would be punished too.

"Then, has it not become clear to them how many generations We destroyed before them as they walk among their dwellings? Indeed, in that are signs for those of intelligence" (Quran 20:128)

God shares these stories in the Holy Koran to warn people about the punishment of nations that disobeyed their Creator, Allah states:

"Have they not traveled through the Earth and observed how was the end of those before them? They were greater than them in power, and

they plowed the Earth and built it up more than they have built it up, and their messengers came to them with clear evidence. And Allah would not ever have wronged them, but they were wronging themselves" (Quran 30:9)

God also states:

"And never would your Lord have destroyed the cities until He had sent to their mother a messenger reciting to them Our Verses. And We would not destroy the cities except while their people were wrongdoers" (Quran 28:59)

It's crucial to indicate God punishes nations when they disobey their messenger while their Prophet is present amongst them. This is because when the messenger invites people to worship the One God, often the rejecters and the deniers would mock the messengers, persecute them, attack them, and sometimes even kill them. They would also sarcastically ask the Messengers of Gods, *'if you were God's messenger, then ask God to send down a punishment to us right now.'* They asked for their punishments to be hastened, so it's only fair they got punished.

In addition, God destroys people when they collectively insist on evil after several repeated warnings. Nations that refused to accept faced God's Wrath and were destroyed, while those who believed in God's Messengers attained the means to everlasting success and salvation. So, read the Holy Quran and take lessons from the stories of the past nations. Reminisce of the nations who reached the pinnacle of civilization, amassing great wealth and power and prestige, only to be ungrateful and forget themselves and their Lord. They became corrupt, arrogant, cruel and oppressive, as they lived ungrateful lives and turned to falsehoods and false gods. God sent to them His Prophets, supported by miracles and revelation, to remind them of His Favors and remind them to be compassionate amongst themselves and His creation at large. But they disbelieved in God the Almighty, despite His Clear Signs and warnings.

Some ruins of past civilians, cities, and nations can still be seen as a reminder today, proof, and a sign to mankind. God is the most Merciful and the Most-

Forgiving. He loves to Forgive. However, God is also All-Just, and His warnings should not be ignored, rejected or denied because God's punishment can be rapid and severe.

MUSLIMS & NON-MUSLIMS

The Arabic word *'Muslim'* literally means someone in submission to the will and law of God. The Message of Islam has always been universal and meant for all people. Anyone who accepts this Message becomes a Muslim. One out of four persons on this Earth is a Muslim. There are 1.8 billion followers which equate to about 24% of the global population. While Islam is the world's second-largest religion, after Christianity, Islam is the fastest growing religion. Muslims are projected to surpass Christians around 2070 as the largest religious group in the world.

While much may associate the religion of Islam with countries in the Middle East, only 18% of Muslims are Arabs & 82% of Muslims are non-Arabs. Muslims represent the majority population in fifty-six countries. The Muslim population is a diverse community of believers spanning the globe. There are many Muslims who live in Europe, South East Asia, & in the West. Islam is not limited to one ethnicity or group of people. Muslims are made up of people from a wide variety of ethnic backgrounds, races, cultures, and national origins. Whereas there are more Christians than Muslims, the religion that has the most followers practicing their faith and its rituals is Islam. There is a higher percentage of Muslims practicing Islam than Christians practicing Christianity.

A Muslim is a person who submits his or her will to Almighty God, as he acknowledges that God knows what's best for him; so, he follows God's commandments for his own best interest. A Muslim is someone who lives to attain a higher purpose in life. A Muslim lives to better himself and the things around him. A Muslim lives following God's commandments so he can live a peaceful and happy life in this world, and so he can prepare himself for eternal joy in the next world.

THE SACRED PATH TO ISLAM | 55

In Islam, worshipping God comprises every act, belief, statement, or sentiment of the heart which God approves and loves. Anything that brings a person closer to His Creator would be considered an act of worship. It includes physical and external forms of worship like the daily ritual prayers that Muslims are prescribed to do, fasting, and charity. It also contains internal worship such as faith in the Angels, God's Books, and His Prophets. Acts of worship also include the loving of God, gratitude, reverence, and reliance on God. God is worthy and entitled to worship by the body, soul, heart & mind.

In Islam, a Muslim is not someone who just knows the truth; a Muslim is someone that submits to the fact. A Muslim is someone that believes in God and Follow God's commands. Islam stresses belief does not just mean believing in one's heart, but also acting on the belief. Mere faith counts for nothing if not carried into practice. The purpose of Islam is not merely knowledge, it is the submission, and no belief or knowledge by itself can bring salvation. Even Satan believes in God as he has spoken to God. The Quran records a dialog between Satan and his Lord:

"He said, "My Lord, then reprieve me until the Day they are resurrected. [Allah] said, "So indeed, you are of those reprieved. Until the Day of the time well-known." [Satan] said, "My Lord, because You have put me in error, I will surely make [disobedience] attractive to them on Earth, and I will mislead them all Except, among them, Your chosen servants" (Quran 15:36-40)

However, Satan disobeyed his Lord and refused, stubbornly and arrogantly to prostrate when his Lord commanded him to which showed a severe nature of arrogance, self-admiration, and pride. The fact that Satan believed in the existence of God without rightful action, did not benefit him. Satan became amongst the disbelievers because his belief was canceled out by his pride, arrogance, stubbornness, and his poor behavior before his Lord. Belief in God and action complement each other and are intertwined. Love manifests itself in action and belief in the heart results in good actions. If a man truly loves God, he would show it in his obedience to God's commandments to earn God's pleasure.

Islam states that both inner beliefs, and outward actions, make up what is known in Islam as *'Iman'* which translates to faith. When Muslims obey God's commandments, it does not deny them pleasures of this world. God made humans the successors of this Earth, God states in the Quran:

> **"And [mention, O Muhammad], when your Lord said to the angels, "Indeed, I will make upon the Earth a successive authority..." (Quran 2:30)**

Islam states humans have been put here on Earth by God and they are to use the material means to build a positive life in this temporary world which will eventually lead them to a positive eternal life in the Hereafter. God states:

> **"But seek, through that which Allah has given you, the home of the Hereafter; and [yet], do not forget your share of the world. And do good as Allah has done well to you. And desire not corruption in the land. Indeed, Allah does not like corrupters" (Quran 28-77)**

Islam does not take the ability and the right to live well in this world. Instead, Islam teaches every experience one has in this world should be more than just that feeding moment. This world is much more than just living to entertain oneself and to accumulate material goods. A Muslim lives for a more superior and compelling reason. A Muslim lives to find purpose in his life and that purpose is to discover who created him, determine how his Creator wants him to live, and to build a relationship with him.

The opposite of a Muslim is a *'Kafir.'* The Quran warns one against being a kafir. The word kafir occurs over 150 times in the Holy Quran. The word kafir refers to something that is covered up or concealed. For instance, a farmer is also called kafir in the Arabic language–because a farmer covers seeds in the earth. The Qu ran uses the word kafir to describe a disbeliever because a kafir is one that is insincere in their life; deliberately rejecting the truth which they covered despite knowing its truth. A kafir is also someone that refuses to question the beliefs taught to them during their childhood. They blindly follow their forefathers without thinking, reflecting and pondering over their beliefs. They do not search for the truth.

The word kafir in the west is usually translated to an infidel which is not the proper definition. The word infidel means someone who does not believe in God, whereas a kafir is someone that denies, conceals, or refuses the truth. A kafir is someone that rejects the truth or knows the truth but refuses to act upon it. A disbeliever is also someone that is ungrateful; who lives, hide, or cover in the darkness of ignorance.

Islam does not teach to hate non-Muslims. Islam came to bring dignity to all human beings. The Quran explicitly states that the children of Adam are honored. God has given respect to all sons of Adam which would include every human. If God gives them respect, we certainly need to respect them. God States:

"And We have certainly honored the children of Adam and carried them on the land and sea and provided for them of the good things and preferred them over much of what We have created, with [definite] preference" (Quran 17:70)

The term 'Children of Adam' which God uses to refer to humanity, excludes any discrimination based on race, color, or gender. Human dignity is universal since all human beings are descendants of Adam. God also commanded His Angels to prostrate themselves in humility before Prophet Adam peace be upon him, the father of humanity, when he was created to elevate the status and honor of humanity. Also, God mentions in the Quran how He has honored the sons of Adams and made them noble by creating them in the best fashion and most perfect forms.

"We have certainly created man in the best of stature" (Quran 95:4)

God is very explicit in the Quran about treating non-Muslims poorly that even if one's parents are idol worshippers and forcing them to worship false gods, one should not worship those gods but should treat their parents with the utmost respect and love.

During the time of our Prophet, Prophet Muhamad peace be upon him was sitting with his companions when a funeral service passed in front of them.

Prophet Muhammad stood up. Then, one of his companions ask him, *'why are you standing? This is the funeral service of a Jew'* Prophet Muhammad replied, *'Was it not a soul?'* He was teaching his companions that all humans are valuable.

Islam teaches that the only real criterion by which one surpasses another is that of piety, God-consciousness in actions, and righteousness.

"O mankind, indeed, We have created you from male and female and made you peoples and tribes you may know one another. Indeed, the most noble of you in the sight of Allah is the most righteous of you. Indeed, Allah is Knowing and Acquainted" (Quran 49:13)

A Muslim is someone that doesn't make wealth, health and power his or her ultimate aims of in life. Whereas Muslims use these to live; it's not their aim or goal. Muslims have a much bigger aim in life than the gathering of perishable material goods.

Since the life of Prophet Muhammad is filled with countless examples that show his status as a role model for humanity for all, including societies and individuals, one can find truths in Prophet Muhammad's life that make up an example for them to follow. His life was full of good manners, superior morality, generously, good habits, politeness, respect, gentleness, noble feelings and wisdom from God, all of which help mankind live a better, peaceful, and more comfortable life full of good.

Emulating the Prophet would also help one from falling into error or sin. Prophet Muhammad is the sacred model for humanity to emulate and follow his footsteps as he was sent by God the All-Generous as an example of how one should live his life to the best of his ability. Thus, Muslims study the Biography of the Prophet Muhamad which they call *Seerah*. Muslims believe the most accessible road to goodness, moral excellence, and success in this life and the afterlife comes through an emulation of the Prophet. Muslims emulate Muhammad's faith, behavior, attitude, manners, patience, compassion, piety, and even daily tasks like the way he ate, drank, slept, interacted with others, etc. The teachings of Prophet Muhamad acts as a mercy and a healing for all of humanity.

A Muslim is someone that continually tries to improve him or herself and tries to perfect his manners. Islam stresses the importance of ethical behavior. A Muslim is one that treats his parents, spouse, children, and family kindly. Islam forbids Muslims from mistreating and being unjust to their parents or family and made it compulsory for one to treat them with all goodness and mercy.

"And your Lord has decreed that you not worship except Him, and to parents, good treatment. Whether one or both of them reach old age [while] with you, say not to them [so much as], "uff," and do not repel them but speak to them a noble word" (Quran 17:23)

Islam incorporates a basic set of rules designed to protect the rights and freedoms of individuals and communities. The Islamic concepts of freedom, human rights, and the ability for one to live in a secure community are embedded in and granted by Islamic law called the Sharia. One of the greatest sins one can commit to Islam is intentionally taking One's life unless it's for a just cause.

A Muslim is one that gives charity, helps the needy, the poor, and orphans. Giving to the needy is not just recommended by Islam; it is required of every financially stable Muslim. Zakat (alms-giving) is an obligation for those who have been blessed with wealth from God to respond to those members of the community in need. A Muslim is one that lives with humility and does not live with pride or arrogance. Nor is a Muslim boastful or vainglorious. Islam condemns pride and self-righteousness.

"And do not walk upon the Earth exultantly. Indeed, you will never tear the Earth [apart], and you will never reach the mountains in height" (Quran 17:37)

Islam teaches Muslims the best way to greet his fellow brother or sister is with the Islamic greeting of *'As-Salam Alaykum'* which translates to *'peace be upon you'* which grants the other for protection, safety, security, and mercy from evils and faults. The name *'Al-Salam'* is one of the names of God in Arabic, so it also means *'May the blessing of His Name (God) descend upon you.'*
No matter what nationality, ethnicity or color a Muslim brother or sister may be, it is an obligation for one to greet his fellow brother or sister as a family

since all Muslims share the belief in One God and the last and final Prophet and Messenger Muhamad.

Muslims are obligated to spread the word of Islam to others which is called *Da'wah* in Arabic. *Da'wah* translates to mean, *'to call or to invite'*. In the Islamic context, the word refers to calling, conveying, inviting people towards the Message of Islam, towards God, towards the Truth, towards the right path prescribed by the Almighty for all of mankind. The call of *Da'wah* invites, inclines, and encourages people to voluntarily submit to the Will of Allah, by worshipping Him alone and following His commandments.

> **"Call to the way of your Lord with wisdom and fair preaching, and argue with them in the best manner possible..." (Quran 16:125)**

Whereas Islam states guidance only comes from God, and no one can embrace Islam except with the permission and will of the Almighty, Muslims are still obligated to convey the message of Islam according to their capacity and circumstance. Muslims also remind, re-educate, and motivate current non-practicing to become better Muslims. According to Allah the Glorious, no one has a better speech than those who engage in calling upon others to his religion and way of life of Islam. The Quran says:

> **"And who is better in speech than one who invites to Allah and does righteousness and says, "Indeed, I am of the Muslims" (Quran 41:33)**

There is no one whose speech is better than that of a person who calls people to the truth, for he is their guide to their Creator and Lord who removes people from their darkness of misguidance into the light of faith.

PROPHET MUHAMMAD

Muslims believe in the same Prophets mentioned in the Jewish and Christian traditions, including Prophet Noah, Moses, Abraham, and Prophet Jesus peace be upon them all. They were sent with the same general Message — to worship God Alone, without partners, sons or daughters and to follow God's commandments. Before Prophet Muhammad peace be upon him, Prophets were only sent to particular people in particular places and periods. However, Prophet Muhammad is the last and final Prophet who is meant for all humankind until the end of time.

Prophet Jesus was sent after Prophet Moses to reform Judaism, to reinstate the rule of the Divine, and to seep away all innovations introduced after Prophet Moses had passed. But Prophet Jesus peace be upon him was rejected by the majority of his people who tried to crucify him. The Israelites and the Roman authorities could not harm Prophet Jesus as God raised him to the Heavens. He departed saying, *'But very truly I tell you, it is for your good that I am going away. Unless I go away, the Advocate will not come to you; but if I go, I will send him to you (John 16:7)* Prophet Jesus peace be upon him was referring to the Prophet that was coming after him, Prophet Muhamad.

Such like how Prophet Jesus came to reform the previous Message sent before him by the previous Prophet, Musa peace be upon him, Prophet Muhammad came to reform Prophet Jesus' Message since it was as well distorted by his followers and did not survive in its original form. Prophet Jesus stated: *"I still have many things to tell you, but you can't bear them now. When the Spirit of truth comes, He will guide you into all the truth. For He will not speak on His own, but He will speak whatever He "hears." He will also declare to you what is to come"* (John 16: 13) Prophet Jesus Christ hinted that God would reveal another Book and Messenger. The man that Jesus Prophesied was Prophet Muhammad, who was the Paraclete, the comforter, the helper, the admonisher sent by God after Prophet Jesus. Prophet Jesus spoke of Prophet Muhammad in John 16:14 stating, *"He shall glorify me: for he shall receive of mine and shall show it unto you"* This Prophecy applies to Prophet Muhammad, to whom was the Holy Quran was revealed to from God to guide people unto the truth.

> **"O our people, respond to the Messenger of Allah and believe in him; Allah will forgive for you your sins and protect you from a painful punishment" (Quran 46:31)**

God speaks to Moses, *'I will raise for them (the Israelites) a Prophet like you from among their brothers (the Israelites); I will put my words in his mouth, and he will tell them (the Israelites) everything I command him.'* (Deuteronomy 18:18) The Christians mistakenly believe this Prophecy refers to Prophet Jesus because Prophet Jesus was like Prophet Moses in a way they were both Jews, and both were Prophets. However, if you are looking at only these two criteria, then all Prophets of the Bible who came after Prophet Moses such as Prophet Isiah, Daniel, Joel, etc. will fulfill this Prophecy since all of them were Jews and Prophets. It is, indeed, Prophet Muhammad who is like Prophet Moses as the verse stated. Both Prophet Muhamad and Prophet Moses had a father and mother whereas, Prophet Jesus had no father. Both Prophets were also married and had children whereas; Prophet Jesus did not marry nor have kids according to the Bible. Both Prophet Mohamed and Moses peace be upon them died natural deaths whereas Prophet Jesus was raised in the Heavens by God.

Prophet Muhammad is from among the brethren of Prophet Moses because Arabs are brethren of Jews. Prophet Abraham had two sons, Ishmael and Isaac peace be upon them. The Arabs are the descendants of Prophet Ishmael, and the Jews are the descendants of Prophet Isaac. Prophet Muhammad was unlettered who didn't know how to read, write, and calculate, so his Revelation would come straight from God verbatim as the verse stated.

Prophet Muhammad peace be upon him was born about 570 years after the birth of Prophet Jesus peace be upon him. He was born in Mecca, in the Arabian Peninsula. The people of Mecca were devoted to idol-worshippers and the area and period at the time were full of ignorance, foolishness, and misguidance. At forty, Prophet Muhammad received his first Revelation in a cave from God via the Angel Gabriel. He then spent the remaining portion of his life explaining and living the teachings of the Holy Qur'an and Islam, the religion that God revealed to him.

Although he was known among his community as 'the truthful, the trustworthy' the majority of his people did not believe him or his Message. Soon after, a massive campaign started to persecute those who believed in the Message. After thirteen years of preaching in the city of Mecca, Prophet Muhamad migrated to the city of Medina, where he gained some followers. The followers made him the leader of the city.

The disbelievers of Mecca plotted and attempted to attack the faith sent from God. However, what was originally a small group of Muslims grew in number, and they could withstand the attack of the disbelievers. Within ten years, the Prophet himself led an army back to Mecca and conquered it in a bloodless victory. Later, Islam spread throughout the World. Prophet Muhammad died in 632. God states in the Quran that He did not send Prophet Muhammad except as a mercy for humanity.

"And We have not sent you, [O Muhammad], except as a mercy to the worlds" **(Quran 21:107)**

The Prophet was sent to guide humanity. Prophet Muhammad understood the Koran, he loved the Koran, and he lived his life based on the principles of the Koran and its standards. He is the World's best role model for all humankind. He is the one with outstanding virtues and characteristics. He was an astonishing husband, father, grandfather, leader, teacher, judge, and statesman. He preached justice, fairness, peace, and love.

Muslims attempt to emulate the Prophet Muhammad's faith, behavior, attitude, patience, charity, compassion, righteousness, and piety. The act of emulating the Prophet is called 'Sunnah' The term 'Sunnah' is a concept that means 'the way,' or 'practice of' The meaning of Sunnah is generally understood as thru act of doing whatever the Prophet said, did, or approve. Sunnah is the way or the practice of Prophet Muhamad. Muslims emulate the way the

Prophet ate, drank, the position he slept on, the way he behaved and interacted with others, etc.

Following the *Sunnah* (the way of the Prophet), would make one's life in this world and the next easier. Islam is such a natural way of life that its rules, regulations, and recommendations become easy to adopt. Islam is not merely a religion; it is a way of life; a holistic approach designed by the Almighty to benefit the one that follows it. The comprehensiveness of Islam allows every intention, word, or action in life to be an act of worship, where one gains reward from the Almighty, from praying to God, giving charity, helping others, eating, drinking or even sleeping.

"There has certainly been for you in the Messenger of Allah an excellent pattern for anyone whose hope is in Allah and the Last Day and [who] remembers Allah often" (Quran 33:21)

Prophet Muhammad is undoubtedly one of the most influential figures in history whose life, actions and thoughts changed the world. When Muslims declare their faith in One God, they also maintain their belief in the last and final Messenger, Muhammad peace be upon him. Muslims believe in Prophet Mohamed peace be upon him, they love him; they respect him; they obey him, and they follow him to the best of their ability. They hold him in such high regard that for many it is emotionally painful to see or hear their beloved Prophet and teacher ridiculed, disrespected, demeaned, scorned, or mocked.

Whereas Muslims look up to Prophet Muhammad peace be upon him; they do not worship or attribute any divine characteristics to him. Certain people mistakenly assume that Muslims worship Prophet Muhammad peace be upon him by formulating a false analogy since Christians worship Prophet Jesus; they presume Muslims worship Prophet Muhammad. Hence, incorrectly naming the followers of Islam to *'Mohammedans.'* Muslims understand that Prophet Muhammad is only a man and was sent from God. Though, Prophet Muhammad peace be upon him is a man worthy of our utmost attention, respect, and love.

The man who will stand before God on the day of Judgement and beg God to have mercy on us. The one that will intercede for us on the day of Judgement.

Muslims love and respect him because he is the slave and Messenger of God who was chosen to be the last and final Prophet whom the Almighty sent to humanity whose mission will continue until the Last Day.

PURPOSE OF LIFE

God is real. He is the One and the Only God. He is worthy of worship and veneration. He is All-Loving. He is All-Knowing, All-Seeing, All-Hearing. He owns everything, including you and I, the Sun, the Moon, the World, everything it contains. He is in control of all things. He wants people to believe in Him, to do good and to avoid evil so they can achieve the reward of Paradise. God sent all of humanity on this worldly journey as a test, to weed out the worthy from the unworthy, to test which of those amongst His servants would perform best. Humanity would be lost on Earth if they were left to their own devices because they wouldn't know what God expects of them. When one acts according to their feelings, desires, and passions, they become oppressed by the sadness, worry, and fear that results from these impulsive actions.

Humans can't navigate the twists and turns of this life without God's Guidance. Humans must ask their Creator for guidance, and to show them the Straight Path. God bestowed Guidance unto His servants in the form of Revelation and through prayer; the form of communication through which Muslims connect with God at least five times a day. The goal of a follower of Islam is to become a faithful servant of God by submitting to His Will and to worship Him Alone. Those who pass this test would enter Paradise eternally; those who fail, meanwhile, would enter hellfire in the afterlife.

Let's take a closer, more in-depth look at this subject. Everything populating the Heavens and Earth, including animals, the Mountains, the Skies, and the Earth, are all in a state of submission to the Sovereignty of Allah, the Glorious. They are all living for, obedient to, in submission to, and are at the disposal of God and His Laws. They all exist in a state of Islam (submission to Allah). God states in the Quran:

"To Him submits whatever is in the Heavens and the Earth" (Quran 3:83)

Everything in nature functions according to fixed laws set forth by God and cannot deviate from those laws. The Sun knows its role---it knows the cycle of its rotation; it knows its role as the giver of light, heat, and energy on Earth. The Earth knows its rotation cycle around its axis. Your own eyes, heart, brain, your entire body and all of its components, are working subject to the laws of nature—and have no choice but to do as they are intended. All of God's creation worships Him in a manner appropriate to their situation. The Sun, the Moon, the Stars, the Mountains, the trees, the animals, the whole Universe all exist in a state of subjugation to Allah, the Almighty. All prostrate to Him, with all of them worshipping Him in an appropriate manner. God, the Almighty said:

"Do you not see that to Allah prostrates whoever is in the Heavens and whoever is on the Earth and the Sun, the Moon, the Stars, the Mountains, the trees, the moving creatures and many of the people? But upon many, the punishment has been justified. And he whom Allah humiliates - for him there is no bestower of honor. Indeed, Allah does what He wills" (Quran 22:18)

Man is expected to worship and praise his Creator, much like the surrounding creations are continuously praising God in humility; in a way we may not understand. All the creation praises, worship, and lives in submission to the Almighty, in their unique style. God's creation prostrates to Him as per its nature, even if they do not press their foreheads to the ground.

"The seven heavens and the Earth and whatever is in them exalt Him. And there is not a thing except that it exalts [Allah] by His praise, but you do not understand their [way of] exalting. Indeed, He is ever Forbearing and Forgiving" (Quran 17:44)

All of God's creations know their mission and purpose. Just like the physical world submits to its Lord, human beings must submit to the Will and Laws of God. Unlike other creations of God, man was gifted with the qualities of intelligence, the ability to comprehend and understand, and the wisdom to think, reflect, and ponder over his Creator and his life purpose. Man was also gifted with the ultimate beauty of expression, and with the ability to make choices and decisions. God created many astounding creations, and the noblest of those creations are human beings. God states in the Quran:

"We have certainly created man in the best of stature" (Quran 95:4)

Man faces a choice: the offer to submit before God like all other creations or to go astray and violate God's laws. All will be held accountable for their decisions and choices.

All humans are born with an innate eagerness and ability to seek God, to recognize and understand the existence of their Creator. Once many discover the truth, they hasten to submit to Allah; entering a state of total submission. Islam answers the questions that trouble the conscience of every human being: *Why was I created? What am I doing here? What is my life's purpose for existence?* Islam answers these massive life questions.

Mankind was also born in a pure and pristine original state; one that inclines toward that which is ethical, morally and spiritually pure, upright and wholesome. They incline to help others, removing objects from the road, thanking people, etc. Everyone has an internal moral conscience, calculator, compass. If it is not corrupted, man's intrinsic moral conscience suffers discomfort and upset when someone wrongs; this because this conscience always points toward good, which brings one closer to God. This goodness, which is programmed in humans, compels them to be grateful when something good comes its way.

Every human has an instinct to believe in and worship a Creator who is One—who has no partners. This belief does not come about as a result of learning or personal reflection but is placed by God into the heart of every human. With time, the changing of one's environment, and outside influences from parents and friends, this innate belief in God affects and confuses a person. Prophet Muhammad narrated: *'Every child is born in a state of fitrah (a natural belief in God), then his parents make him a Jew, a Christian, or a Magian.'* (Saheeh Muslim)

Humans have the eagerness to thank their Creator. God has reinforced man's natural disposition with the signs He has planted throughout creation, to testify to His existence. A primary aim of the Holy Qur'an is to invite people to ponder and reflect. Allah refers to the Earth, the Sun, the Moon, the merging of the night into the day, and the merging of the Day into Night, as His miraculous signs and evidence of an existence of a Creator.

The Quran teaches that the signs and proofs of God's knowledge, Wisdom, Power, Mercy, and existence are evident in the world around us. Together they point to a Creator, a Maker, a Designer, a Fashioner. This creation is flawless and perfect. Life on Earth and the Universe itself demonstrates so much order, purpose, intelligence, and design; all of which prove the existence of a Creator that designed and fashioned everything.

Thus, God calls on man to ponder, reflect, and think deeply about the design of this complex creation, to build a better understanding of his Creator. When one reflects, one realizes that the world and everything it contains was created with intelligence and Infinite Wisdom—not by chance.
Human beings—regardless of who they are, where they are, and when they live—are always curious to why they exist in this world, for what purpose? Only our Creator can tell us why we are here, and for what purpose!

God encourages one to observe and ponder over His beautiful creation. He asks man to reflect upon the Mountains, the Sun, the Moon, the Stars, the Trees, etc. so they will realize their blessings. They will witness a clear sign, evidence, and proof of His existence, look up to the sky and admire the beauty of the ocean, mountain, and sunset:

Have they not looked at the heaven above them - how We structured it and adorned it and [how] it has no rifts? (Quran 50:6)

One should ask him/herself when was the last time he/she admired and pondered over this beautiful creation?

Recognizing the signs of God's existence would require personal effort, and this recognition occurs in accordance with his or her wisdom and conscience. For the people who understand, everything around them is a sign and evidence of their creator's existence. Pondering upon the intricacy and order of this magnificent creation would help one conclude that this glorious Universe indeed has a Wise Creator who crafted, fashioned, and molded everything. One would eventually perceive the fact that the entire Universe, including oneself, and one's own body, is created by a Superior Power. One would conclude that this world was created in proportion, and with measure and definite purpose.

"And We did not create the heaven and Earth and that between them for mere play" (Quran 21:16)

God also encourages people to look at their creation, their own body, and how it was constructed so perfectly.

"We will show them Our signs in the horizons and within themselves until it becomes clear to them that it is the truth. But is it not sufficient concerning your Lord that He is, over all things, a Witness?" (Quran 41:53)

Pondering over the creation of mankind and the Universe would help one realize that the Deity behind this ethereal creation can re-create it once again. One would understand that God can easily and quickly resurrect all of humanity for Judgement Day.

"How can you disbelieve in Allah when you were lifeless, and He brought you to life; then He will cause you to die, then He will bring you [back] to life, and then to Him, you will be returned" (Quran 2:28)

In today's materialistic world, the endless quest for fame and wealth distracts many from reflecting on the beautiful creation of God and the purpose behind it. We live in a world where people are obsessed with materialism, and their main aim and focus in life is to gather all the money and prizes they can. We are in a world where people are obsessed with taking as much as possible from this world. A perpetual state of excessive materialism can affect one's inner peace. One cannot achieve satisfaction in life if he or she is chasing material gains to an excessive and extreme extent; rather, one should look at the situation of those who are less fortunate. In this way, one will have a greater appreciation of the love, gifts, benefits and mercy that the Almighty has bestowed upon them regarding their wealth, family, friends, housing, etc.

Humanity was created and born with a sense of awe, of wonder, but many have killed that sense of wonder somewhere along his or her journey to adulthood. Many no longer feel the fear and awe at God's creation around them because of their excessiveness, obsession and distraction of materials of this world. Many are so occupied by useless material goods, vain talk, and gossip they have forgotten and are immune to the miracles happening around them every second of every day. One should think deeply and ask more significant questions about life and his/her purpose, rather than thinking of that which is less significant.

For the few that ponder and think deeply on this creation, which others overlook, they discover within it signs and great lessons all around them that lead them straight back to their Creator. Signs that lead one to an appreciation of the Wisdom and Wonders of the Almighty's creation, bringing them thus closer to their Lord. In the Holy Koran, God invites individuals of understanding to think about the issues which other people overlook.

"Praise be to God. He will show you His Signs, and you will recognize them. Your Lord is not heedless of anything you do" (Quran 27:93)

A person's purpose in life is to find God, build a relationship with Him, and engage in a continuous effort to submit to His will. The best joy and the most peace that one can achieve in this world is derived from the servitude to God and being an obedient slave of God. God states unequivocally that humankind was created to worship Him. God states:

"And I did not create the jinn and mankind except to worship Me" (Quran 51:56)

One can easily misunderstand this to mean that God wants humans to be in constant prayer, to dwell on the remembrance of God at all times, and to spend their entire lives in constant seclusion and absolute meditation. This is not the case. In Islam, worshipping God includes and entails every act, belief, statement, or sentiment of the heart which God approves and loves. The act of worship in Islam is comprehensive in scope. The worship of God can include actions such as removing an object from the road, helping one in need, being kind to one's parents, lawfully making money, sharing food with neighbors, visiting an ill person, etc. The act must be done sincerely to please God and not with boastful or impure motives. The action should also be consistent with the Almighty's guidance and laws. Any thought or act that brings a person closer to his Creator would be considered an act of worship.

To worship God is to get to know Him, learn His names and attributes, to love Him, to obey His commandments, and to enforce His laws in every aspect of life. To worship God is to serve His cause; engaging in the struggle and the quest of doing right, shunning evil, and being just to others.

According to the Quran, following and obeying God's commandments and refraining from prohibited activities would make one's life easier, more comfortable, and lighten one's burdens.

"And Allah wants to lighten for you [your burden/ difficulties], and mankind was created weak" (Quran 4:28)

Some mistakenly believe that disobeying the commands of God while partying their whole life away would make for a more enjoyable, peaceful life. They also think if they find God and follow His commands, then they will deprive themselves of things they could have otherwise enjoyed—and this couldn't be further from the truth. Quite the opposite is true. While the commands of other religions are often viewed as burdensome and rigid, the rules of Islam are not seen this way by the devout Muslim. A devout Muslim would see these rules as what's best for him or her, so that they may be guided to success, happiness, honor, and contentment in this life and the next.

God states that if you abide by his advice, He will relieve the burdens of your life, rendering your existence much easier, comfortable, and more relaxed. You would find contentment in the heart. You would find more peace and harmony, not only within yourself but with the things and people around you. Each of God's commandments is enforced to benefit the one that follows them. Anything that God makes impermissible is harmful to one or society. For example, alcohol is prohibited in Islam because of its danger and evilness. A lot of studies and evidence demonstrate the effects and risks of drinking alcohol.

Those who follow these simple edicts will enjoy a pleasant, contented life in a blessed world. God promises in the Holy Quran:

"Whoever does righteousness, whether male or female, while he is a believer - We will surely cause him to live a good life, and We will surely give them their reward [in the Hereafter] according to the best of what they used to do" (Quran 16:97)

God created particular desires within the human being. One can control these desires according to God's Law or to turn them loose and go his or her separate way. Allah, the Glorious, created humanity knowing that they would sin. Therefore, God taught humans, starting with Prophet Adam peace be upon him how to repent and purify self of the sin.

Life in this world is also a test for humankind. Everyone faces a separate and unique test. Some get tested through a life of poverty; some are tempted by wealth, some enjoy good health, some suffer from bad health, etc. God states in his Holy Book:

"[He] who created death and life to test you [as to] which of you is best in deeds - and He is the Exalted in Might, the Forgiving" (Quran 67:2)

At times, the Almighty tests His creation with calamities and sometimes with blessings, to show who will be thankful and who will be ungrateful, and to show who will obey and who will disobey.

"And We will surely test you with something of fear and hunger and a loss of wealth and lives and fruits, but give good tidings to the patient" (Quran 2:155)

God is testing every individual. God tests all of humanity in different ways. One should not mistake his/her life problems for punishments; or as signs that God is displeased with him or her. Likewise, one never should interpret his or her wealth, previsions, and pleasures as signs that Allah is pleased with them, or that they are privileged. Sometimes, quite the opposite is true. Allah also says:

"Know that your wealth and your children are but a trial and that Allah has with Him a mighty reward" (Quran 8:28)

God in His Wisdom and Mercy has decreed that people be tried and tested in various ways to develop their psyches, strengthen and improve their character, and evolve them into beings which are pleasing to Him. Sometimes when one undergoes certain instances of suffering, he/she immediately thinks about and prays to God even if he' s/she's not religious. At times, the very experience of suffering leads one to God.

A Muslim view this world as a temporary stop en route to a final destination: the afterlife, where man would live eternally. Not that this temporary world is not important or shouldn't be taken seriously, but this life should not be lived sinfully and at the expense of the Hereafter—which is a lot longer and better in scope. If one's goal in life is to become wealthy, then there would be no purpose in existence after one achieves the goal of wealth. How could wealth then be considered the aim of life? This world is not about acquiring material goods or physical pleasures.

A Muslim view and interacts with this world for what it is, just a means to an end. Detachment from this world doesn't mean that you abandon all material possessions and own nothing substantial; instead, a healthy detachment from this world means that nothing should hold, own, and enslave you. This life is about attaining a higher purpose. One should be preparing for the eternal joy of the afterlife. The purpose of life in Islam is to become faithful, sincere servants of God.

"And this worldly life is not but diversion and amusement. And indeed, the home of the Hereafter - that is the [eternal] life, if only they knew" (Quran 29:64)

This life is temporary and will someday end for the individual, and an end for humanity altogether; but the Hereafter is eternal. The experience of life in this world is almost nothing compared to life in the Hereafter. Prophet

Muhammad peace be upon him stated: *'What is the example of this worldly life compared to the Hereafter other than one of you dipping his finger in the sea? Let him see what he brings forth.'*

Whereas the essential purpose for which humankind was created is embodied in the worship of God, God does not need human worship. He certainly did not create human beings out of a need to seek His Glory. If not a single person worshipped God, it would not diminish His Glory. God exists with no needs. On the other hand, humanity was created with needs and wants. Thus, it is mankind that requires the worship of God. Human beings need to worship and glorify God by obeying his divinely revealed laws; because obedience to God is the key to success in this life and the Hereafter.

Mankind is encouraged to remember God as often as possible for their benefit. Remembrance of God is imperative, as sin is generally committed when God is forgotten. The forces of evil operate most freely when cognizance of God is weak or lost.

"Satan has overcome them and made them forget the remembrance of Allah. Those are the party of Satan. Unquestionably, the party of Satan - they will be the losers." (Quran 58:19)

It's Satan and his children that seek to occupy one's mind with irrelevant thoughts, material distractions, and desires that make them forget their Lord.

"O, believers! Remember God often." (Quran 33:41)

The Almighty instructs man to show gratitude to Him by glorifying Him.

"Glorify the praises of your Lord and be of those who prostrate [to Him]" (Quran 15:98)

In glorifying God, man is in harmony with the rest of the creation; an act which naturally Glorifies the Creator throughout the day and night, in its own and unique matter.

Since it is not possible for mankind to have a detailed knowledge of God, and to know what God expects of them without Divine Revelation, God sent His Messengers throughout the ages, to every nation, to guide and educate people about their Creator; advising them how to worship Him, and how one should live his/her life. The Messengers came bearing a Holy Book from the Almighty. All Messengers and all Books preached the same general Message that there is no deity worthy of worship except Allah—who has no flaw and is all worthy of praise and gratitude.

HADITH & SUNNAH

The Holy Quran is the primary Source of Islam and the literal Spoken Word of God. The Holy Quran is the only Book in the world which contains the exact and pure word of God Himself. Hadith, meanwhile, is the second source of Islam. Unlike the Quran, the statements known as Hadith was created and preserved by humans and not directly by God.

While Prophet Muhammad peace be upon him was practicing and preaching the teachings of Islam and the Koran to his companions; his companions would report and record the statements, actions, and beliefs of the Prophet. The companions of Prophet Muhammad peace be upon him gathered them, and later by scholars who specialized in Hadith. These reports then were collected and known to be called Hadith.

In the Arabic language, Hadith, or A'Hadith in its plural form, has several meanings. Hadith translates to mean speech, narration, report, or news. In the context of Islam, Hadith refers to a narration or report that Prophet Muhammad peace be upon him said, did, or approved. Hadith can also refer to the Prophet's reaction or silence in response to something said or done by others. Hadith is a body of reports that makes up speeches, discourses, statements, actions, sermons, teachings, sayings, and approvals of the Prophet. Hadith also contains accounts of Prophet Muhammad's behavior, physical features, and character traits. Hadith also contains theology, doctrine, law, ethics, morals, manners, and more. Hadith also comprises a commentary of the Holy Quran, which would help a reader understand the Holy Quran better. Hadith helps answer questions regarding details and specifics of the religion.

The acts and practices of the Prophet are called Sunnah. Prophet Muhammad stands as the sacred model for humanity to emulate and follow, as God sent him as an example of how one should live his or her life.

"There has certainly been for you in the Messenger of Allah an excellent pattern for anyone whose hope is in Allah and the Last Day and [who] remembers Allah often" (Quran 33:21)

The term Sunnah comes from an Arabic root word which means to *'pave the way'* making a path easier, more comfortable, and more accessible as in it becomes commonly followed by many in its wake. The term *'Sunnah'* is usually interpreted as *'the act of'* or *'example of the Prophet.'* Muslims study and ponder over the Hadith text to benefit from the prophetic knowledge transmitted to mankind in the form of these narrations.

Hadith is preserved through acts of memory, practice, and writing. Hadith was taught from a teacher who learned it from his teacher, and ultimately can be traced back to the companion who took it from Prophet Muhammad peace be upon him; together, these people form the chain of narrators. The words and actions of the Prophet are found in different books of Hadith. While Hadith is criticized, and some fabricated Hadith stems from people with hidden agendas, no criticism is leveled at the Quran as it constitutes the exact word of God and is separate from Hadith. Hadith was passed down and preserved with human intervention, as opposed to the Quran; which God guarantees to protect from all manner of human modification.

Hadith is composed of two parts: the *'Isnad'* and the *'Mat'n.'* The *isnad* refers to the chain of people who narrated the particular Hadith. The *isnad* must be comprised of upright and sincere individuals, whose integrity is unquestionable. Scholars of Hadith impose strict qualifications on these narrators, to ensure that every member of the chain of narrators is qualified to tell and pass down the story of the Hadith. If one lacks credibility, then the Hadith would be rejected.

The second part of Hadith is the *Mat'n*, which is the actual text of the narration.

Like Hadith, the Bible contains reports from individuals; however, the authors of the reports provided in the Bible are unknown. The reporters of the Hadith are all known people, credible, honest individuals, who have established its chains of narration.

Muslims do not follow the way of the Prophet as though he was some demigod. Prophet Muhammad was a mere human being whom God chose to be His last and final Prophet.

> Say, "I am only a man like you, to whom has been revealed that your God is one God..." (Quran 18:110)

God commands people to follow His Prophet. Hence, following the way of the Prophet is akin to acting in obedience and submission to Allah, the Glorious.

> "O, you who have believed, obey Allah and obey the Messenger and those in authority among you. And if you disagree over anything, refer it to Allah and the Messenger, if you should believe in Allah and the Last Day. That is the best [way] and best in result"   (Quran 4:59)

Prophet never bespoke his desire. He spoke only those words sent down to him from his Master when conveying the Message.

> "He does not speak out of his own desires" (Quran 53:3)

ARTICLES OF FAITH

To become a Muslim, each follower must believe in six Articles of Faith (which translates to the word Iman in Arabic). These six articles of Faith form the foundation of the Islamic belief system. The six articles of Faith are:

Belief in the Oneness of Allah
Belief in the Angels of Allah
Belief in the Prophets & Messengers of Allah
Belief in the Books of Allah
Belief in the Last Day & Judgement Day
Belief in Divine Predestination

Linguistically, the Arabic term *'Iman'* or *'faith'* in English, comes from a root word which means to give safety, to give security; *Iman* makes one feel safe and secure. Without Faith, one would fall into a state of despair. The root word of Iman means to believe in the truth of something or someone, with this belief imbuing you with a genuine sense of peace. One would believe to a level and an extent he or she is certain that belief is true, which gives them peace and contentment. One must believe God's tenets and teachings, verbalize those concepts with their tongue and manifest God's teachings in their actions. Believing in and relying upon God will lead one to find safety, security, and contentment even in times of hardship, as one would acknowledge that he or she is not alone, and that God is with them at all times and fully knows of their situation.

Muslims are asked to believe in that which they never saw with their own eyes, which is the very essence of Faith itself. Belief in God is something natural for humans. Humans by nature are believers in God, as belief in God is inherent to each.

"Indeed, those who fear their Lord unseen will have forgiveness and a great reward"
(Quran 67:12)

ONENESS OF GOD

The first article of faith in Islam presents the belief in the Oneness of God. Iman (or faith in English), begins with the belief in Allah, the Glorious, from which all other facets of faith spring. A Muslim must adhere to and acknowledge the idea that no deity is worthy of his or her worship, love, subservience, hope, and fear, other than Allah. Nothing in existence is worthy of one's ultimate loyalty and sacrifice nor worth the lowering the head in prostration or humility, except for Allah, the Creator of All. The Arabic word *Allah* means God. Allah is not a different God, nor a new God invented by Prophet Muhammad or by Muslims. Allah is the semantic term for God. Arabic Jews and Arabic Christians also use the word Allah in their Books.

Islam is a monotheistic religion, and the belief that only One God should be worshipped is fundamental to the faith. The idea of multiple gods is rejected in Islam, as is highlighted many times throughout the Qur'an.

**"They have certainly disbelieved who say, 'Allah is the third of three,'
And there is no god except one God. And if they do not desist from
what they are saying, there will surely afflict the disbelievers among
them a painful punishment" (Quran 5:73)**

In another verse, God expresses His wrath for those that attribute a son to Him; calling it highly inappropriate and atrocious for one to commit this sin.

**"And they say, 'The Most Merciful has taken [for Himself] a son' You
have done an atrocious thing. The heavens almost rupture therefrom,
and the earth splits open, and the mountains collapse in devastation.
That they attribute to the Most Merciful a son. And it is not**

appropriate for the Most Merciful that He should take a son" (Quran 19:88-92)

The most severe sin in Islam is known as *shirk*, which translates to the concept of ascribing a partner to Allah. The term also encompasses attributing divine qualities to any other besides Allah. Shirk is the only sin that God does not forgive if a person dies before repenting from.

The Christian belief that Jesus is the son of God, or God himself, is an example of shirk. The belief in the concept of the Trinity--father, son, and holy spirit— is a grave sin in Islam. Allah states in the Holy Quran that on the Day of Judgement, Prophet Jesus peace be upon him will deny ever asking people to worship him instead of God or along with God:

"And (remember) when Allah will say (on the Day of Resurrection): 'O 'Jesus, son of Mary! Did you say unto men: 'Worship me and my mother as two gods besides Allah?' 'He will say: 'Glory be to You! It was not for me to say what I had no right (to say). Had I said such a thing, You would surely have known it. You know what is in my inner-self though I do not know what is in Yours, truly, You, only You, are the All-Knower of all that is hidden and unseen" (Quran 5:116)

God is the One to whom worship is due; He is the Creator, the Provider, the Sustainer of everything. He is the Supreme, the Eternal. God has no father nor mother, no son or daughter, no partner nor equal. He is All-Knowing, All-Seeing, All-Hearing, All-Powerful, All-Merciful. It is He who gives life and causes death; it is He who is Unique in His Names and Attributes.

Everything in this world and everything it contains, the whole universe, including you and I, belong to the One God. We use the phrases, 'my hand,' 'my house,' 'my money,' but in reality, it all belongs to God.

"To Allah belongs whatever is in the heavens and whatever is in the earth. Whether you show what is within yourselves or conceal it, Allah will bring you to account for it. Then He will forgive whom He wills and punish whom He wills, and Allah is over all things competent" (Quran 2:284)

ANGELS

The second article of faith that a Muslim must embrace is the belief in the Angels. The Angels are part of the unseen world which we cannot comprehend and cannot prove scientifically. One cannot see the Angels unless God allows for and enables their vision. Muslims believe in Angels because they are mentioned numerous times throughout the Holy Quran, and in the sayings of the Prophet Muhammad peace be upon him; a body of work which Muslims call Hadith.

"The Messenger has believed in what was revealed to him from his Lord, and [so have] the believers. All of them have believed in Allah and His Angels and His Books and His Messengers..." (Quran 2:285)

God describes the appearance, attributes, characteristics, and responsibilities of Angels in His Holy Book, The Quran. We do not know of precisely when Angels were created, but they pre-date the creation of human beings. The Angels are created from pure shining light (Noor in Arabic). They are light-giving entities. The Angels are generally more powerful than humans and travel the speed of light. The Angels have certain specialties and capacities that humans do not possess. God refers to the Angels as honored servants.

"...Rather, they are [but] honored servants" (Quran 21:26)

In Arabic, Angels are called 'Mala'ika', which means 'to assist and help.' Angels are Holy and exist in a constant state of worship and praise to God all day and all night and do not disobey Him. They worship Allah constantly, without growing bored or tried.

"They exalt [Him] night and day [and] do not slacken" (Quran 21:20)

The sole purpose of the Angels (*Mala'ika*) is to execute the commandments of Allah. The Angel has no needs or desires for material goods. The Angels do not eat, drink, sleep, marry, or procreate. The Angels do not die. The Same Angels that existed when Prophet Adam peace be upon him was created still exist today and will continue to live until the trumpet is blown for the Day of Judgement. A countless number of Angels exist, a number so high we can't comprehend its scope in our finite minds. Only God knows. We learn from a narration of Prophet Muhammad that there is a sacred heavenly House in the 7th Heaven called *Al-Bayat Al-Mahmoor* (The Much-Frequented House). This House is directly above the *Kaaba*, the Scared Black Cube in Najd (known as Saudi Arabia today). Every day a new group of 70,000 Angels circle this house, leaves, and never returns; being followed by the next group of 70,000 Angels. God states in the Quran:

"...And none knows the soldiers of your Lord except Him..." (Quran 74:31)

The Angels (*Mala'ika*) have no gender; they are not female nor male. Angels are physically very beautiful, expect the Angel for the guardian of the hellfire, who wears a stern expression and never laughs. The Greatest of Angels are magnificent in size, far beyond our imagination. The largest and most significant of all Angels is the Angel Gabriel (Jibril in Arabic), who is the Angel that descended from Heavens to instruct the Prophets how to teach and preach their religion. All Angels have wings; some possess 2, 3, or 4 pairs of wings or more. Angel Gabriel has 600-wings and is of a size so great it fills the space between Heaven and Earth, blocking the entire horizon.

The Angels (*Mala'ika*) that carry Allah's Throne possess such a substantial capacity that the distance between the Angel's ear-lobes to their shoulders is equivalent to a 700-year journey. Most Angels reside in the Sky, and we learn that there is not a single space in the Sky of four fingers long, except where an Angel is occupying that space, worshipping and praising their Lord. Angels can take on different forms, including a human form like the Angels that visited Prophet Abraham and the Virgin Mary peace be upon them.

Angels (*Mala'ika*) have different status, rank, and categories. Some Angels are of a higher level than others. Islam does not teach the concept of fallen or evil angels. Nor does Islam teach the idea that humans transform into angels after death. Islam also does not teach Angels are the children of the Almighty.

The Angels (*Mala'ika*) are servants and messengers of God, who serve His kingdom in full obedience and complete submission. Some angels are assigned the duty of executing God's law in the physical world. Angels surround humanity at all times, but mankind does not see them. There is a group of Angels that continuously record mankind's deeds; known as the *'honorable scribes.'* Each person is assigned to two Angels, which record every single good and evil deed by that individual; not a single word or deed is left unrecorded.

There is a group of Angels that make supplication for those that give charitably, or who teach and spread the word of Islam. Angels love the believers and supplicate to and beseech God to forgive the believer's sins. Amongst them exists Angels that protect the believer throughout his life, whether he is at home, traveling, or asleep. Angels have been assigned different tasks and duties in the unseen and physical worlds. A group of Angels is recorded by name in the Holy Quran and Sunnah (Hadith), which include:

Angel Gabriel (Jibreel): Responsible for communicating Allah's Revelation to His Prophets

Angel Mikael (Mekaeel): Responsible for directing rain, food, crops, and sustenance with the Will of God.

Angel Raphael (Israfeel): Responsible for blowing the trumpet to mark the Day of Judgment

Angel Maalik: Leader of the Guardians/Gatekeepers of the Hellfire

Angel Munkar & Angel Nakir: Responsible for questioning people in the grave after death

Angel Harut and Angel Marut: Who were sent to the people of Babylon to test their faith

Angel Ridwan: Guardian of Heaven

Angel of Death: (Malak Al-Maut): Responsible for taking possession of souls from bodies after death by the Will of God

Other Angels (*Mala'ika*) are mentioned in Islamic text, but not specifically by name. The Angels are not to be worshipped, prayed to, or supplicated to, or to be taken as objects of praise or veneration as they are not divine or semi-divine. Nor do Angels deliver prayers to God. The Angels (*Mala'ika*) are merely in submission to God and carry out His commands. A Muslim recognizes that Angels are but a creation of God. Indeed, God is in no need of the Angels' assistance and does not need to be worshipped or revered by the Angels or humans, as he is a free and independent Deity who gains nothing from the worship of others.

"To Allah belongs whatever is in the heavens and earth. Indeed, Allah is the Free of need, the Praiseworthy" (Quran 31:26)

It's imperative that one learns about the Angels (*Mala'ika*) so that one can ponder, reflect and reaffirm over the Greatness of his/her Creator. The experience of having knowledge and belief in the Angels (*Mala'ika*) adds to the awe that one feels towards God, in that He can create this great being; and indeed, can create whatever He Pleases and Wills. The awe and magnificence of the Almighty's creation reveals and indicates the Magnificence, Glory, and Majesty of the Almighty Himself. This should humble the human being and increase one's God consciousness and love and fear of the Almighty. Knowing of the Angels (*Mala'ika*) would also remind one that his actions are continuously being recorded by Angels which hopefully decrease one's sins and increase good deeds.

GOD'S SCRIPTURES

Muslims are obligated to believe in all Inspired Books that God has sent down to serve humanity, as delivered through His Prophets. Every Prophet received Inspiration from God. Some Revelations were later compiled to form the content of larger Books such as the Holy Quran, Gospel, Torah, and the Zabur.

The Arabic word for Inspiration or Revelation is *Wahi* which has several meanings. Wahi means an idea or something revealed or written, commandment, suggestion, to point out something, or to send a message. Inspiration or Revelation comes to God's Human Prophets either directly or through an intermediary of the Angel Gabriel, who brings the Revelation to them. Every religion that believes in God believes in Revelation.

God's Books to mankind contain Commandments of God, prohibitions, exhortations, stories, parables, reminders, descriptions of Himself and His Attributes, descriptions of the afterlife, Heaven and Hell, the purpose of life, the creation of the Universe, Worship, Piety, morals, manners, the importance of being kind to one's parents, and much more.

These Books seek to guide man through every aspect of life. God's Books act as a guide, an instructional manual regarding how one's life should be lived. God, in a high manifestation of His Mercy, Compassion, and Love, sent Books to teach and guide humanity.

"...Your Lord is the possessor of vast Mercy..." (Qur'an 6:147)

Islam counts as an article of faith the belief in all of God's Books, in their original, pure form.

"Say, [O believers], 'We have believed in Allah and what has been Revealed to us and what has been Revealed to Abraham and Ishmael and Isaac and Jacob and the Descendants and what was given to Moses and Jesus and what was given to the prophets from their Lord. We make no distinction between any of them, and we are Muslims [in submission] to Him'"
(Quran 2:136)

Unfortunately, the modern-day texts of the Torah and Bible have been altered by men and contain mixtures of humanmade ideas and innovations that corrupt their current state. Whereas these Books still contain some remaining traces of truth, they do not stand in their original revealed form. God warns in his final Testament, the Holy Quran:

"So, woe to those who write the 'scripture' with their own hands, then say, 'This is from Allah,' to exchange it for a small price. Woe to them for what their hands have written and woe to them for what they earn"
(Quran 2:79)

When previous Holy Scriptures were altered and corrupted by human hand, God in his Mercy enlisted his last and Revelation, the Holy Qur'an. God has taken it upon Himself to safeguard & protect his final Book to humanity from human-made alterations or any form of corruption.

The Holy Quran is the only scripture in existence today that exists in its original language and words. Not one letter of the Quran has been changed since its Revelation. The Holy Quran is meant to serve and teach all people until the end of time. Everything found in the Quran is truth, with no evidence of contradictions or falseness, and will remain so for eternity.

Muslims believe that the Koran has abrogated all previous Scriptures before it; meaning it cancels the rulings of the earlier scriptures and renders them inapplicable going forward since the preceding scriptures were meant for the earlier nations and not for us. God, in his infinite wisdom, did not feel fit to send down the Holy Quran at the time of previous nations. As the Creator of the World and everything it contains, God knows who is capable of understanding and who is not. Although different revelations came down to various Prophets and nations, the general Message had always remained the same: 'To worship God Alone and to follow his Commandments.'

The Quran mentions the following Books by name:

Torah was sent with the Prophet Moses (Musa in Arabic) to the Children of Israel

Psalms (Zabur in Arabic) was sent with Prophet David (Dawood in Arabic) to the children of Israel

Gospel (Injeel in Arabic) was sent with Prophet Jesus (Isa in Arabic) to the children of Israel

The Scripture Revealed to Prophet Abraham

The Holy Qur'an was sent with the last and final Prophet, Muhammad to our nation, which is the last nation, to all of humanity. No other scripture will be revealed after it.

PROPHETS & MESSENGERS

Believing in God's Prophets and Messengers is a fundamental part of Islam. Muslims believe God sent Prophets and Messengers to convey his Message to humanity. The Holy Quran states:

"And We certainly sent into every nation a messenger, [saying], 'Worship Allah and avoid Ta'ghut (false deities).' And among them were those whom Allah guided, and among them were those upon whom error was [deservedly] decreed. So, proceed through the earth and observe how was the end of the deniers" (Quran 16:36)

Every people, every nation was given a Prophet, and they were sent with the tongue of their people. Muslims believe that Prophet Muhammad is the only universal Prophet meant for the whole Globe since he is the last and final Messenger. All other Prophets and Messengers including Prophet Moses and Prophet Jesus peace be upon them were only sent for a particular group of people/tribe who lived before us. Islam states all Prophets came with the same general Message to Worship Only One God and Follow His Commandments. Whereas some finer details differed from one nation or Book to another, the Theology and God never changed.

Due to God's Mercy and Love to humanity, God continued to send Prophets and Messengers to deliver give good news and warning to their people. The general Message was whoever worships the One God and follows His commandments will go to Paradise for eternity. And whoever worships other than Allah and goes against His Commandments will enter the Hell Fire. The Prophets also came to teach their people how to purify oneself. Every Messenger was given Inspiration from God. Some of those Inspirations were written down and complied to become more extensive Books.

The Prophet & Messengers that God sent to humanity to convey His Message cannot make mistakes for speaking on behalf of God. Humanity could not attain true knowledge of morality and ethics without the knowledge from their Creator to reveal what is truly good and evil. Muslims believe that God communicates His guidance through human Prophets. These Prophets were sent to guide their people, not only by preaching people to worship the One God and follow His commandment but by example with their actions.

A *Messenger (Rasool in Arabic)* has a higher rank than a *Prophet (Nabi in Arabic)*. A Messenger is sent to a tribe or people that did not believe in the Message and generally sent with a new Revelation (Divine Laws). A Prophet (Nabi in Arabic) is someone that was sent to a people or a tribe that already believed in the Message and carried and continued the same Revelation from the prior Messenger before Him. Every Messenger is a Prophet, but not every Prophet is a Messenger by default. The Islamic Tradition states there are about 124,000 Prophets that were sent to people and nations and 310 and some Messengers. There are 25 Prophets mentioned by name in the Holy Quran.

1. Prophet Adam
2. Prophet Enoch (Idris in Arabic)
3. Prophet Nuh (Noah)
4. Prophet Eber or Heber (Hud in Arabic)
5. Prophet Methuselah (Saleh in Arabic)
6. Prophet Abraham (Ibrahim)
7. Prophet Lot (Lut in Arabic)
8. Prophet Ishmael (Ismail in Arabic)
9. Prophet Isaac (Ishaq in Arabic)
10. Prophet Jacob (Yaqoob in Arabic)
11. Prophet Joseph (Yusuf in Arabic)
12. Prophet Job (Ayoub in Arabic)
13. Prophet Jethro (Shuaib in Arabic)
14. Prophet Moses (Musa in Arabic)
15. Prophet Aaron (Harun in Arabic)
16. Prophet Ezekiel (Dhul-Kifl in Arabic)
17. Prophet David (Daud in Arabic)
18. Prophet Solomon (Suleiman in Arabic)

19.   Prophet Elijah (Ilyas in Arabic)
20.   Prophet Elisha (Al-Yasa in Arabic)
21.   Prophet Jonah (Younus in Arabic)
22.   Prophet Zachariah (Zakariya in Arabic)
23.   Prophet John (the Baptist), (Yahya in Arabic)
24.   Prophet Jesus (Isa in Arabic)
25.   Prophet Muhammad

Peace be upon them all.

Muslims believe all Prophets and Messengers were mere human beings, not divine or semi-divine. They do not have the right to be worshipped, adored, revered, venerated and nor did they claim so.

BELIEF IN THE LAST DAY, RESURRECTION, & JUDGEMENT DAY

To mark the World's end, God the Almighty will order Angel Israfil to blow a trumpet to announce the arrival of this fateful Day. At the blast of the trumpet, a blast will be heard so horrendous and terrifying that the inhabitants of the Heavens and the Earth will fall unconscious, except those whom Allah wills. The Mountains will be lifted, crushed and crumbled into pieces likening wool, the sky above will split open and crack piece by piece, the Oceans will boil over as they burn in flames. The Planets, the Moon, the Stars will fall from their orbits, losing their shine. Darkness will commence everywhere. The Earth will shake in a terrifying quake, flattening and leveling with no peaks or troughs. Every living thing will cease to exist.

"Then when the Horn is blown with one blast, And the Earth and the mountains are lifted and leveled with one blow, Then on that Day, the Resurrection will occur" (Quran 69:13-15)

Then Allah will command His Angel to blow the trumpet for a second time, and a violent earthquake will erupt, causing the graves to split open and all of the creation from the beginning of time will be resurrected.

"And the Trumpet will be blown (i.e. the second blowing) and behold! From the graves they will come out quickly to their Lord" (Quran 36:51)

Then God will replace this Earth and Heavens with another creation. Every deceased person will rise up from their grave, reclaiming their original physical body. Bones and body parts will be reassembled in their original form. Just as God created the everything the first time, he will do so again.

"The Day when We will fold the heaven like the folding of a sheet of paper. As We began the first creation, We will repeat it. [That is] a promise binding upon Us. Indeed, We will do it" (Quran 21:104)

People will rush from their graves so quickly in chaos, terrified and confused. A child's hair will turn grey and their face will wrinkle from fear. A nursing mother will forget her child, and pregnant women will miscarry. People will run about in chaos as if in a drunken state, but they are not drunk, but the punishment of Allah is severe.

"They will say, 'O Woe to us! Who has raised us up from our sleeping place?' [The reply will be], 'This is what the Most Merciful had promised, and the messengers spoke truth' (Quran 36:52)

On this Day, a man will flee from his brother, mother, father, spouse, and children nearest and dearest to him, even as they beg for help. Man will think only of himself, terrified as his soul peers into the eyes of infinity.

God will gather all mankind naked, bare-footed, and uncircumcised, including both the believers and non-believers, all jinn (spirits made from smokeless fire), and all animals, all of whom will be brought to a plain known as the place of gathering. No one will speak, and heads will be lowered in humility as they hear only footsteps.

"And they will be presented before your Lord in rows, [and He will say], 'You have certainly come to Us just as We created you the first time. But you claimed that We would never make for you an appointment'" (Quran 18:48)

Everyone will be stripped of the titles and roles which they held in their worldly lives. The kings, the presidents, the millionaires, the poor, the slaves, all will be lined before their Lord regardless of the ranks and classes they possessed throughout the course of their worldly lives. The area will be so overcrowded, with humans, jinn, and animals all pressing each other, that every individual would be crowded into the space covered by their own two feet. People will stand nervously waiting for judgment, and mankind will perspire in agony. Anxiety levels will run so high that not a single person will sit down on that frightening Day.

As humankind awaits the decree of the Almighty, the sun will descend so low above their heads, it will linger a mile away and each person will sweat according to the level and intensity of their good and bad deeds. Some will sink to their own ankles in their own perspiration, while others would sink to their thighs and waist, and still others would drown in their own sweat, flowing up to their mouths. The only souls that will be shaded will be seven categories of righteous people who will be granted shade during this traumatic day in which there will be no other shade but the shade of Allah's Magnificent Throne.

On this Day, Allah the Exalted will gift Prophet Muhammad a pond called the pond of Kaw'thar; one located in the courtyard of the place of gathering, where the water is whiter than milk and sweeter than honey. He will drink from the pond and invite the Believers and the righteous of his nation—those who died in the way of Allah and His Messenger—to drink from the same pool. A personal invitation will be required to drink, and Prophet Muhammad will recognize the righteous of his nation by the foreheads, hands, and limbs rendered bright and shiny from the effects of their wudu (ablution that is performed before prayer to remove impurities of the body). Those who reach this pool will drink from it and quench their thirst permanently.

"Indeed, the righteous will be among shades and springs" (Quran 77:41)

Judgment Day will equal 50,000 years in duration of our time, but for the believers, it would only feel like the time elapsed between the Asr to the Maghrib prayer, which is a roughly a couple of hours.

For the unbelievers and the wrongdoers, conditions on this Day will be intense and unbearable, this because of the terror, the heat, the standing, and the thirst prevalent during this period. All of mankind, including Muslims, Christians, and Jews from all nations, would unite and some would exclaim, *'Let us ask somebody to intercede for us and ask our Lord to begin the accountability.'*

Then all of mankind will rush to Prophet Adam and ask, *'O Prophet Adam; you are the father of all mankind, whom Allah created with his own hands, please intercede for us.'* Prophet Adam then will respond, *'Myself, Myself, I am not fit for this. I fear the same thing you fear as I disobeyed my Lord once, and today my Lord is in the state of anger which He has never been before. Please go to Prophet Noah!'* Then mankind will go to Prophet Noah, who will respond the same to the effect, *'Myself, Myself, I cannot do this, go to Prophet Abraham!'* Then mankind will go to Prophet Abraham, then to Prophet Musa, then to Prophet Jesus. Prophet Jesus then will respond, *'I am not fit for this as people took me for a God and I have to answer to that.'*

Finally, all of mankind will reach Prophet Muhammad, who will respond, *'This is what Allah has favored me for and the only intercession I'll be able to give is on behalf of my nation who followed me. As for the nations before me, they will need to go after their Prophets; and as for the disbelievers and for the ones that worshipped other than Allah, they will need to follow those who they followed and worshipped in their worldly life.'* Prophet Muhammad will then prostate to His Lord and will praise His Lord with words inspired within him by God. God, the Almighty then will say, *'O Muhammad, lift your head and ask for anything and I will give you.'* Prophet Muhammad then will respond, *'O my Lord, save my nation, save my nation.'* Then Judgement will begin.

God will call upon each individual to stand before Him, to judge and question him/her according to his or her faith and how they lived their life, with no translator or interpreter needed. The conversation will involve only you and Your Master, who will judge you and your deeds. Each individual will be held accountable for every action they took, said, and intended, all of which were recorded inaccurate records by each person's assigned Angels.

The first thing that will be questioned is whether each person performed their mandatory prayers. Each individual will be asked terrifying questions about how he/she lived their life, utilized their youth, earned and spent their wealth, and what One did with the knowledge they acquired. One will be reminded and informed of the good and bad deeds they have done. On that Day, one would either meet the Mercy of God or the Justice of God.

As the disbelievers will try to argue and lie their way out of their deserved punishment, God will seal their mouths, hands, feet, ears, skin, and body parts;

with these body parts testifying against them as surprise witnesses of their life actions. Their body parts will complain to God, their Master, on how that person made them sin.

"**That Day, We will seal over their mouths, and their hands will speak to Us, and their feet will testify about what they used to earn.**" (Quran 36:65)

The disbelievers will ask their own body parts why they bore witness against them, to which they then will reply, *'God, who gave speech to all things, has made us speak.'* Everyone shall be dealt with according to their deeds and actions. No injustice or transgression will occur on this Day, not even for the disbeliever or the evilest of people.

When the Reckoning is completed, books of each records and deeds will fly to each person. Everyone will be given his or her Book, that will contain records of all the deeds he or she performed in their life.

"**And then the record of their deeds shall be placed before them and you will see the guilty full of fear for what it contains and will say: 'Woe to us! What a Record this is! It leaves nothing, big or small, but encompasses it.' They will find their deeds confronting them. Your Lord wrongs no one**" (Quran 18:49)

The believer will be given his Book in his right hand, as a sign of honor. The One who will receive his record in his right hand will undergo an untroubled audit. His sins will be overlooked, and he will turn to his people rejoiced.

"**As for him who is given his Book in his right hand, he will say, 'Here! Take and read my Book! Indeed, I was sure that I would have to face my Reckoning (one day), So he will have a pleasant life, in an elevated garden, whose clusters [of fruits] will be within easy reach, [He will be told]: 'Eat and drink pleasantly for what you did before in the days gone by'** (Quran 69:19-24)

As for the disbeliever, the wrongdoer, he or she will receive their book in their left hand or from behind their back, receiving the worst kind of auditing with full regret, wishing he or she were dead as they anticipate their descent into the Hellfire.

"But as for he who is given his record in his left hand, he will say, 'Oh, I wish I had not been given my record And had not known what is my account. I wish the death (that I suffered in the world) was the final death. My wealth has not availed me, and my power has perished from me.' [It will be ordered], 'Seize him and shackle him. Then into Hellfire drive him. Then into a chain whose length is seventy cubits insert him.' Indeed, he did not use to believe in God, the Most-High, nor did he encourage the feeding of the poor. So there is not for him here this Day any devoted friend. Nor any food, except from the discharge of wounds; none will eat it except the sinners." (Quran 69:19-37)

Then the scales intended for weighing people's deeds will be presented for view. A balancing scale which is real and accurate in its results. No act, even of an atom's weight of importance, will be overlooked, whether it took the form of cursing, backbiting, stealing, or something that was done or said for the good of helping someone.

"And We place the scales of justice for the Day of Resurrection, so no soul will be treated unjustly at all. And if there is [even] the weight of a mustard seed, We will bring it forth. And sufficient are We as accountant" (Quran 21:47)

A person's good deeds will be placed in one pan, and his evil deeds in the other. If his good deeds outweigh the evil, then—with God's Mercy—success and salvation will be rewarded for that individual. If one's evil deeds outweigh his good deeds, then he or she would be condemned to the Hellfire for severe punishment.

"And the weighing [of deeds] that Day will be the truth. So those whose scales are heavy - it is they who will be the successful. And those whose scales are light - they are the ones who will lose themselves for what injustice they were doing toward Our verses (Quran 7:8-9)

Then Allah will destroy all lights and pure darkness will fall everywhere, so dark that if one placed his hand in front of his face, he could not see it. Paradise will lie on one side and in order to reach it, one would have to cross a very narrow bridge. A bridge so narrow, it would stand thinner than a hair and sharper than a knife; under the bridge will burn Hellfire. People will need to pass this bridge with the aid of his or her light, which would shine from their bodies in accordance with their belief and the righteousness they presented in their lives.

And there is none of you except he will pass over it. This is upon your Lord an inevitability decreed (Quran 19:71)

Some people will reflect very strong bright lights emanating from their bodies and will pass the bridge in a blink of an eye. Every act of worship accepted by God will be transformed into light on that Day. Our Prophet stated, *'Convey glad tidings to those who walk to the Mosque in the darkness. For they will be given full light on the Day of Resurrection'*

Others will emanate only enough light to see one step ahead, some will crawl, and some will fall into the Hellfire. This slippery bridge has thrones, and hooks that will snare people, and the soul will struggle and fight against the fall. The ones that do not deserve to pass the bridge will fall. And those who successfully cross the bridge will approach Paradise. The Prophets will wait on the other side, praying to God to save their nations. Amongst the people will stand the Hypocrites who will ask the believers to share their lights, so they can pass over the bridge and they will be told in response, *'Get your own light.'*

"On the [same] Day the hypocrite men and hypocrite women will say to those who believed, 'Wait for us that we may acquire some of your light.' It will be said, 'Go back behind you and seek light.' And a wall will be placed between them with a door, its interior containing mercy, but on the outside of it is torment" (Quran 57:13)

The final stage before the admission to Paradise is what's known as the *Gon'ta'ra*, where one would have to make amends with people they harmed or wronged in their life—those to whom they never made amends or of whom they never asked forgiveness. If a person were wronged and did not receive justice from his abuser, he finally would see justice by benefitting from some of that person's good deeds, which would adjust the level of Paradise they enter.

On the Day of judgment, 70,000 Angels will conjure the Hellfire and every single person will ponder and reflect on the quality of his/her life. But of what purpose will this remembrance and recounting serve at that point? Those who fell into worship of false deities, those who denied the belief of God, and those who lived a wicked and evil life of sin, will be condemned eternally to the Hellfire. They will be led into the Hellfire by the idols and false gods they followed and worshipped to receive their everlasting torture, punishment, pain, and disgrace.

The Hellfire is a place of an unimaginable and immense suffering, extreme blazing temperatures, an unquenchable thirst, a residence prepared for the disbelievers. They will feel remorse and terror as they beg for safety and forgiveness, but it will be too late.

"Indeed, We have warned you of a near punishment on the Day when a man will observe what his hands have put forth and the disbeliever will say, 'Oh, I wish that I were dust! (Quran 78:40)

As for sinful believers, they will be placed into the Hellfire in accordance with their sins—but only to be cleansed from all their sins and eventually sent to Paradise.

As for the ones that believed and worshipped God Alone and lived a righteous life, they will be rewarded generously and warmly welcomed to God's Paradise; where they will live eternally in a garden of physical pleasures and spiritual delights, where every wish shall be granted.

"And give good tidings to those who believe and do righteous deeds that they will have gardens [in Paradise] beneath which rivers flow. Whenever they are provided with a provision of fruit therefrom, they will say, 'This is what we were provided with before' And it is given to them in likeness. And they will have therein purified spouses, and they will abide therein eternally (Quran 2:25)

The people of Paradise will live in beautiful mansions, where rivers will flow beneath them. They will know no disease, sickness, hardship, pain, sorrow or animosity, as God will remove all ill feelings from people's hearts. A place of riches, servants, streams of wine that does not intoxicate, milk that never changes in flavor, honey of utmost purity pleasant in color, taste, and smell, water which does not brackish, pleasant fragrances, and pure, gorgeous partners. Never will a person of Paradise ever feel tiredness, exhaustion, boredom, nor will they ever have to taste death again. The believers will be rewarded with the greatest bliss of all, which will be the honor of looking upon the Holy and Beautiful Face of God, the Glorious. The unbelievers will be deprived of this vision.

"...Say, the enjoyment of this world is little, and the Hereafter is better for he who fears Allah..." (Quran 4:77)

Faith in the last Day, Resurrection, and Judgment Day are fundamental beliefs that Muslims must hold to complete their faith. Everything the Almighty creates and does has a purpose, including the creation of each of our lives. God states in the Quran:

"Did you think that We created you for no reason and that to Us you would not be returned?" (Quran 23:115)

God proves life after death as stated in the Holy Quran. Amongst his proofs is a moral and ethical argument. Certain evil people in this world have gotten away with horrific crimes, and good people have lived difficult lives. If a person was wronged and did not see true justice in his or her life, God will give him his justice on that Day. Without Judgement Day, un-convicted mass murderers would never be punished, and life would be unfair. Everyone shall be judged, and justice shall be served. God states in his Book:

"Do the evildoers think that we will make them like those who believed and done righteous deeds in their life and in their death? Bad, indeed is their judgment!" (Quran 45:21)

If God created mankind the first time, why couldn't He create mankind a second time? To re-create mankind a second time will be even easier. Mankind has already witnessed the Almighty's first creation, in which people were created out of soil:

"And he makes comparisons for Us, and forgets his own (origin and) Creation: He says, 'Who can give life to decomposed rotten bones?' Say, 'He will give them life Who produced them (the) first time; and He (is) of every creation All-Knower'" (Quran 36:78-79)

The creation of the heavens and Earth is greater than the creation of mankind. He, who can create such a vast, and complex world can certainly raise the dead.

Amongst Allah's signs of life after death is the continuous Resurrection of plants and vegetation. Every year we observe the phenomenon of dead land with no vegetation, with the land being dead in the winter only to return to life in the spring.

"And He (is) the One Who sends the winds (as) glad tidings before His Mercy, until, when they have carried clouds - heavy, We drive them to a dead land then We send down from it the water then, We bring forth from it all (kinds) of [the] fruits. Thus, We will bring forth the dead so that you may bear this in mind (Quran 7:57)

God asks man to ponder over the situation of seeds placed on the ground. When water and Earth surround the seeds, they logically should decompose— as opposed to opening and splitting into a root that grows out of the ground, producing magnificent life forms like trees and plants. These are all signs of Allah's Power, Infinite Wisdom, and the Capabilities of bringing about life after death.

The Holy Koran has over 40 names of Judgement day. Among its names is the Day of Standing; since everyone will be too nervous to sit, the Day of Accounting, the Day of Sorting Out, the Day of Eternity, the Day of Meeting, and the Hour. Judgment day will be such a heavy, difficult day that every page of the Quran mentions Judgement Day, either directly or indirectly.

The Quran contains many vivid descriptions of Judgement Day. It's a true blessing that one can acquire knowledge about Judgement Day and its severity now, so he or she can prepare themselves adequately for this Great Day. The possession of faith in life after death encourages one to do righteous deeds, to fear God, to increase his God consciousness, and to avoid wrongdoing.

"O, you who have believed, protect yourselves and your families from a Fire whose fuel is people and stones..." (Quran 66:6)

Do not stand amongst people that have convinced themselves that Judgment Day is far away and that they don't have to prepare themselves for this fateful occurrence.

"O, you who have believed, fear Allah. And let every soul look to what it has put forth for tomorrow - and fear Allah. Indeed, Allah is Acquainted with what you do" (Quran 59:18)

BELIEF IN AL-QADAR
(PRE-ORDAINMENT OR PREDESTINATION)

The last pillar of the Islamic faith in which every Muslim must believe is the concept of *Al-Qadr*, which closely translates to pre-ordainment (or predestination/ Divine Decree, destiny, fate). When one believes in the tenet of Al-Qadr, which we'll translate as 'Divine Decree,' he or she affirms that everything good or bad that happens in his or her life comes from God the Almighty; something He Willed to happen. Al-Qadr in Arabic linguistically means to measure, to determine, to assess, to decide, to judge. In the context of Religion, the term translates to 'Divine determined measurements and sustenance for everyone and everything, in accordance with His Wisdom and Power.' God states in his Book:

Indeed, all things We created with predestination (Quran 54:49)

God the Almighty, being All-Knowing and All-Wise, knows of what we have done in the past, what we are doing now, and what we will do—even before the time of our birth. After all, can God truly be God if He didn't know everything, including the future? Whereas mankind has the free will to make their own choices in life, everything that occurs in life occurs only with the Will and Power of God.

Al-Qadar comprises four components. The first component is the belief that God is All-Knowledgeable of and instigates all things and events—whether major or minor—at all times and places and regardless of their occurrence. The Almighty's foreknowledge is infallible and complete.

"And with Him are the keys of the unseen; none knows them except Him. And He knows what is on the land and in the sea. Not a leaf falls

but that He knows it. And no grain is there within the darknesses of the Earth and no moist or dry [thing] but that it is [written] in a clear record" (Quran 6:59)

The second component of Divine Decree is the belief that Allah has recorded everything from the beginning of time to the Day of Judgment, in a Tablet He has kept known as the *'Lawh Al-Mahfooth' (The Preserved Tablet)*. Each's lifespan, amount of substance, deeds, happiness, sorrow, and more is written and recorded in this Tablet. In fact, according to a narration of Prophet Muhammad peace be upon him, Allah, the Glorious, had recorded the measurements of all matters pertaining to His creation fifty thousand years before He created the heavens and earth.

"Do you not know that Allah knows what is in the Heaven and Earth? Indeed, that is in a Record. Indeed that, for Allah, is easy" (Quran 22:70)

The third component of Divine Decree is the belief that nothing can occur without the Will and Power of Allah, whether the event stems from the action of the Almighty or actions of humanity. Nothing Occurs Haphazardly; the Almighty has planned everything.

"And your Lord creates what He Wills and Chooses..." (Quran 28:68)

A Muslim acknowledges that whatever has touched or afflicted him, was meant to afflict him, and could not have been avoided or prevented. And whatever has not reached or afflicted him, was not meant to touch or afflict him, and he can avoid nothing unless God has willed it. Our Prophet peace be upon him narrated, *'Know if all of humanity gathered to harm you, they could not harm you unless Allah had decreed. The Pen has been lifted, and the pages have dried.'*

The fourth and last component of Divine Decree is the belief that Allah is the Creator and Originator of all things.

"...and has created each thing and determined it with [precise] determination."
(Quran 25:2)

Whereas Allah, the Merciful, has bestowed on every human being the free will to make his or her own decisions, that does not provide an excuse for one to sin or abandon the tasks and responsibilities they are obligated to do. The fact that God has predestined everything does not change the fact that human beings have the free will to choose their course of actions. Just because each's choices are known to God beforehand, doesn't mean that they will not be held accountable on the Day of Judgment for the decisions they make and actions they take. God forces nothing upon anyone. It's also important to note that God will hold no one accountable for things out of their control, or for things they cannot do.

Allah is All-Just, All-Wise, and He tests humanity according to their strength and what their soul can bear. A Muslim acknowledges the fact that whatever difficulty they are facing will be made easy for them and that they will have a way to resolve it.

"God does not burden any human being with more than he is well able to bear."
(Quran 2:286)

A Muslim acknowledges that whatever befalls him or her, is in accordance with God's Will and Plan, whether or not they understand and accept this fact. A Muslim place his trust and reliance in God, as God brims with Wisdom in all matters. A Muslim affirms that God is All-Loving and loves His servants over one's parents do; and a Muslim affirms that whatever God does must have a good motive, so a believer always assumes good and does not lose faith.

The topic of Divine Decree will never fully be understood and comprehended by humans, as this concept deals with the essence of God's Power and Will— which is beyond what our finite minds can comprehend.

A Muslim benefits from the act of learning, believing, and understanding in Divine Decree in several ways. Amongst the benefits is the peace of mind and contentment in the heart that a Muslim attains as he or she acknowledges that nothing happens without a purpose. A Muslim is confident that whatever afflicted him could not have escaped him, and whatever missed him could not have reached him, as God is in full control of all happenings and events, and he predestines everything. This recognition would help a believer endure difficulties and hardships. A believer would not grieve about what could have happened if things had taken a different course, and a believer would not worry about the future because he knows that the events of tomorrow are written and predetermined already.

The act of learning and believing in Divine Decree increases one's belief in, the trust of, and reliance on God, and increases one's likelihood of performing good deeds. Faith in Divine Decree decreases one's pride and arrogance, as he acknowledges that his intelligence and actions did not emanate from him and that God is the source of all that comes his way. Belief in Divine Decree makes a person refrain from fearing anyone else; inspiring his bravery as he acknowledges that no one can afflict harm on him without the Permission and Will of God. Without a strong belief in God, the human learns, life would not be worth living.

5 PILLARS OF ISLAM

T he Religion of Islam is based upon Five Primary Foundations or Pillars. Just as a building would lack stability without the presence of strong pillars, a believer's relationship with God would lack a focus and a secure connection without the observance of and adherence to these five fundamental Pillars.

These Five Pillars or religious duties are mandatory; every Muslim is expected to follow and enact them with utmost devotion. Failure to comply and enact any of these dictates can lead to the commission of grave sin, some resulting even in the expulsion of a believer from the fold and faith of Islam.

These Five Pillars are mentioned individually throughout the Holy Quran and through narrations of Prophet Muhammad peace be upon him which are known as Hadith. The Five Pillars of Islam are:

Testimony of faith in the Oneness of God (Allah) and the last and final Prophet, Muhammad
Establishment of the Five Mandatory Prayers
Concern and almsgiving to the needy (Zakat in Arabic)
Fasting during the month of Ramadan (for Self-purification)
The Pilgrimage to Makkah (at least a once in a lifetime journey for those who can make and can afford it)

The first pillar, the declaration, and testimony of faith rank as the first of these vital, integral Pillars. The remaining principles relate to putting faith into action, as Muslims are required to apply their faith in behavior and practice. The other four Pillars are religious acts are to be performed either daily, once a year, or at least once in a lifetime toward the attainment and accomplishment of faith.

Similar to the Ten Commandments, these Pillars provide a spiritual foundation and a framework to facilitate a Muslim's life. Fulfillment of these Five Pillars provides blessings and rewards for the one following them, in both this life and the next. These Pillars help one establish a closer relationship with their Creator and build a spiritual connection with Him. A faithful Muslim prioritizes these Pillars over all worldly matters, principles or regulations in his or her life, as they form the foundation and starting point for all other good deeds and acts of worship to their Creator.

DECLARATION OF FAITH

The first of the Five Pillars of Islam is the *Declaration or Testimony of Faith (called Shahada in Arabic),* to which every Muslim must adhere. The word *Shahada* in Arabic linguistically translates to *'testifying, bearing witness.'* The Shahada is the Islamic creed. The Shahada contains two parts, both of which a Muslim must testify to and believe.

The first part requires the believer to testify that no deity is worthy of worship, veneration, or complete devotion, other than Allah. A Muslim acknowledges that Allah has the exclusive right to be worshipped, venerated, loved, inwardly and outwardly, by one's heart, tongue, and limbs. A Muslim accepts Allah as the only God, Master, Lord, and Ruler. Allah is not a foreign God, as Allah is the Arabic name for God. Islam states that God has none partners or associates in worship. No other deity, being, or idol is worthy of worship. The act of worshipping any other besides Allah is the biggest sin in Islam; standing as the only sin that is not forgiven if a person dies in that state without repenting.

Regretfully, many have regarded certain historical figures as their gods and deities, who are wrongfully worshipped and venerated; whether they are idols, superstitions, saints, ideologies, ways of life, or any authority figures who claim to be divine or semi-divine--even though they themselves are creations and have no power to bring any benefit or harm to anyone.

"But they have taken besides Him gods which create nothing, while they are created, and possess not for themselves any harm or benefit and possess not [power to cause] death or life or resurrection" (Quran 25:3)

The belief in worshipping the One God is considered the central Message of all of God's Prophets and Messengers, who were sent to humanity to deliver His Message. This was the Message of Prophet Adam, Prophet Noah, Prophet Abraham, Prophet Moses, Prophet Jesus, and Prophet Muhamad; peace be upon them all.

"And We certainly sent into every nation a messenger, [saying], 'Worship Allah and avoid false deities...'" (Quran 16:36)

Through verbally stating these words, believing in them, acting and living upon them, one enters the fold of Islam. Merely saying these words verbally without action does not complete a Muslim.

The second part of the testimony requires the believer to testify that Prophet Muhammad is the Messenger of God. In accepting Prophet Muhammad as the 'seal of the Prophets,' one affirms the belief that his Prophecy confirms and fulfills all the previously revealed Messages beginning with Prophet Adam. Peace be upon him. Whereas Muslims believe in all the previous Messengers and Prophets of God, Islam states Prophet Muhamad is both a Messenger and Prophet of God; one who carries a higher role than all previous Messengers and Prophets before him. Prophet Muhammad was a mere mortal with no share in Divinity, who was chosen by God the Almighty, as the last and final Prophet to the last nation, our nation.

"Muhammad is not the father of [any] one of your men, but [he is] the Messenger of Allah and last of the prophets. And ever is Allah, of all things, Knowing" (Quran 33:40)

A Muslim is required to fully carry out in practice the instruction given by Prophet Muhammad, as commanded by God the Almighty. Prophet Muhammad also serves as the best role model for mankind that ever-stepped foot on Earth, by his exemplary life. Muslims are encouraged to attempt to follow and emulate Prophet Muhammad's examples, manners, generosity, good habits, politeness, respect, gentleness, noble feelings, and way of life to the best of their ability, reflecting an emphasis on Islam and the Holy Quran.

"There has certainly been for you in the Messenger of Allah an excellent pattern for anyone whose hope is in Allah and the Last Day and [who] remembers Allah often"
(Quran 33:21)

These two phrases are the most frequently repeated words in the world, as hundreds of millions of practicing Muslims repeat these words dozens of times throughout their day and through their prayers. It is recommended for a believer to say it when they first rise in the morning and before going to bed. These words reflect and encompass every dimension of a Muslim's life.

The Shahada (testimony of faith) is by far the essential aspect of Islam, as it affirms the belief in the Oneness and Uniqueness of Allah, upon which the whole Religion of Islam is built upon, and all other beliefs hinge. It is the central belief that a Muslim adheres to his entire life. Verbally stating these words and living by them is unquestionably the most significant and most important duty of a Muslim. Unless one acknowledges this testimony, he or she cannot be a Muslim.

Muslims strain to utter these words as their last spoken before departing this world since whoever does so has been promised the destiny of God-given Paradise. However, only the ones that lived and acted upon these words will be granted the ability to utter these blessed sentiments in the form of their final words.

RITUALIZED ISLAMIC PRAYER

The second Pillar of Islam is the mandatory round of ritual prayers that every Muslim must perform five times every day. The Islamic method of Prayer is a ritualized form of worship, which involves the recitation of Verses from the Holy Quran and supplications to God; all while standing, bowing and prostrating. This mandatory act of worship is called *Salah* in Arabic and differs from the act of merely praying or supplicating to God in an impulsive act, just speaking one's mind. Instead, the Salah prayers demand a formalized structure in which one prays a certain way at specific times, as demonstrated to us by Prophet Muhammad peace be upon him; drawing direct inspiration from Angel Gabriel, who learned from God Himself.

The Arabic word *'Salah'*, which is generally translated as Prayer in English, is linguistically derived from the Arabic word meaning *'connection'*; in that this mode of Prayer connects the servant with his Creator. Salah is a Muslim's way of establishing direct contact with God the Almighty. Salah represents a Muslim's affirmation of servanthood and submission to his Creator's Will. In Salah, a Muslim acknowledges his weakness and neediness by seeking and begging for God's guidance, mercy, grace, and forgiveness.

Salah, or this Islamic ritualized Prayer, is one form of worship amongst many in this beautiful faith. However, Salah holds an extraordinary status in Islam because Prayer builds a relationship between a servant and his Creator. Salah is considered the center pole of the Religion of Islam; whoever demolishes or denies this practice in their life, demolishes his or her Religion. According to Islamic Scholars, this is the only form of worship which—if neglected—would exclude the disobedient from the folds of Islam.

When prayer time arrives, one is expected to discontinue their present activity and pray to connect with God, the All-Merciful; refreshing his/her faith for his or her benefit. The act of Prayer helps to remind one why they are here in this world and for what purpose. Prayers help direct a person's thoughts and actions away from sin; from that which is not beneficial. Prayers redirect a believer's thoughts to the remembrance of God.

The Salah prayer is specifically a human form of worship. All other creatures of God, including animals and plants, submit without question to the Almighty in their unique way. Everything in the Sky and Earth declares Allah's perfection and worships Him in their way; a way in which we humans may not understand. All other creations of God are in continuous glorification, praise, and remembrance of God, and worship in their own way. Just like the other members of creation-worship Allah, man is expected to worship God.

"Do not you see that Allah - glorify Him whoever (is) in the Heavens and the Earth and the birds (with) wings outspread? Each one certainly knows its Prayer and its glorification. And Allah (is) All-Knower of what they do" (Quran 24:41)

Humanity was created for Prayer and Divine worship. God states in the Quran:

"And I did not create the jinn and mankind except to worship Me" (Quran 51:56)

God commands humanity to establish and perfect their Prayer, by praying properly with concentration and the utmost humility. Every Muslim must work and practice to improve their prayer technique, which is a lifetime commitment. Muslims must engage in a lifelong effort to master this art of communication with their Creator. The ones that fall into a habitual routine, reciting their words without concentration and humility, would miss the point of Prayer; not benefitting from their Prayer nearly as much as those who pray earnestly and with full concentration and mindfulness.

Neglecting mandatory Prayer is a grave sin in the Islamic faith. Allah, the Glorious shares a dialogue in the Holy Koran in which the residents of

Paradise ask the people of the hellfire as to the reason for their condemnation and that condemned respond:

"They will say, 'We were not of those who prayed, nor did we used to feed the poor, and we used to indulge in vain talk with the vain talkers, and we used to deny the Day of Recompense, Until there came to us the certainty'"(Quran 74:43-47)

The state of one's Prayer will be the first thing that will be asked of each on the Great Day of Judgement. If one's Prayers was in order, then everything else will fall into place. If one's Prayer was not in order, then he will be doomed. The Messenger of Allah stated: *'The first of man's deeds for which he will be called to account on the Day of Resurrection will be Salat. If it is found to be perfect, he will be safe and successful; but if it is incomplete, he will be unfortunate and a loser..."* (At-Tirmidhi).

Prayer should be directed only to God the Almighty, as he is the Only One in full control of everything—including man's destiny. He is All-Powerful, All-Wise, All-Knowing, All-Hearing, and can fill anyone's needs and remove all of man's pain and miseries.

The Islamic ritual of Prayer expresses submission to God, showing humility to, devotion toward, and love of God. Praying to the Creator daily is the best way to build a personal connection with Him while seeking His guidance, Blessings, and Forgiveness. Muslims pray to God to gain spiritual strength and peace of mind and to strengthen the foundation of their faith. A Muslim temporarily steps out of his/her daily activities five times a day to connect to God; to stay mindful of Him in this world of stress, struggle, and distractions. Prayers remind Muslims that Allah is in control of all things so they can put their worldly concerns into perspective.

The Islamic prayer method and mode act as a spiritual diet. Such as the body requires food and water throughout the day, our spirit needs to partake in the remembrance and worship of God to stay spiritually healthy; is not the soul more valuable than the body?

When someone does another person a favor or helps them, it's human nature to want to thank that individual for their aid. Since God has blessed humanity with a countless number of favors, including one's wealth, health, family, and gifts of all kinds, a Muslim prays numerous times to thank Him throughout their day and night. The best way to demonstrate gratitude is through these five daily prayers.

The Islamic ritual prayers come with many benefits—in this world and the next—for the ones that engage in them sincerely and mindfully, with concentration and humility. Amongst the benefits of praying is that the act guards and protects a believer from sins and evil doings.

"Recite what has been revealed to you of the Book and establish the Prayer. Indeed, the Prayer prevents from the immorality and evil deeds, and surely (the) remembrance (of) Allah (is) greatest. And Allah knows what you do" (Quran 29:45)

When one becomes lackadaisical in their worship or neglects Prayer altogether, he or she will experience the consequence of feeling distant from God; which may cause increased instances of sinning and evil doing. As they distance themselves from Prayer and the remembrance of God, they become easier targets for Satan to reach out to and tempt them. The one that guards and faithfully practices his prayers would be mindful of everything else that matters. The one that neglects his prayers would be neglectful of what matters in this life.

Amongst the many benefits of Prayer is the transformative power that Prayer has on a person. Prayer transforms a person's attitude, behavior, mentality, thoughts, and priorities; redirecting these elements to what really matters in life. Prayer softens one's heart towards Allah and his Creation. Muslims that are steadfast in their Prayer is continually looking to help others and have a genuine concern for them—not just themselves.

If one does not see the benefits and positive effects of their prayers, one should question their sincerity, humility, and concentration in praying. God references the fate of past generations who did not take advantage of their prayers—wasting them.

"But there came after them successors who neglected prayer and pursued desires; so, they are going to face Destruction" (Quran 19:59)

Salah (Prayer) is also connected to the state of our Ummah (Muslim community). If our Prayer is strong, then everything else in the state of our community will be healthy. Prayer solves those many problems our nation is facing.

Much like the pillars of a building, where one cannot move them and need to walk around them physically, a Muslim's life revolves around their five daily prayers; instead of casually trying to fit their prayers into their life. A Muslim's prayers are always their top priority in life; everything else comes secondary.

The five obligatory daily prayers for Muslims are:

- Fajr Prayer: From dawn to right before sunrise
- Zuhr Prayer: Just after noon (mid-day, when the sun passes the median point in the sky)
- Asr Prayer: Late part of the afternoon (halfway between noon and sunset)
- Maghrib Prayer: Directly after sunset
- Isha Prayer: Late evening, dark night (approximately an hour and a half after sunset)

The five daily Prayers set the rhythm of a Muslim's day. Prayers must be performed at their appointed due times unless a reasonable excuse exists to delay them. Prayers are prohibited to be postponed to where they overlap into the next Prayer's timeframe.

Before the Prayer is begun, a Muslim is required to perform *ablution (wudu in Arabic)*, which is the act of cleaning and purifying oneself from any physical bodily fluids such as blood, urine, or any impurity with water. The ritual of ablution comprises washing one's hands, face, arms, head, and feet. It's essential that a Muslim must be clean and free of impurities in his body, clothing, and the area in which the Prayer will be performed. One drop of waste matter present anywhere would void one's Prayer.

Prayers can either be performed individually or in a congregation with others at a Mosque (a Muslim place of worship) which is highly recommended for males.

In Muslim countries, Prayer is publicly announced to the community—not by bells—but by an Islamic chant or call of Prayer known as *Adhan* in Arabic. Prayer is commenced by standing up facing the direction of Mecca, in present-day Saudi Arabia, where the Holy House of God—known as the *Kaaba*—is situated. Muslims from all over the globe face the direction in which the first house was built for the worship of the One God. It's important to note that Muslims do not worship the Kaaba; instead, Muslims only use the Holy House as a direction to face while worshipping the One God, as instructed by God Himself.

During Prayer, Muslims are directed to disconnect themselves and clear their minds of any worldly matter as they are conversing with God. They pray to a God who is near, who is All-Loving, All-Hearing, All-Caring, All-Powerful. A Muslim is to concentrate on their words and humble themselves only to the Almighty. A Muslim affirms that God is the Master and that he or she is the servant and slave of God who needs the Almighty's direction, help, and guidance to the straight path. The Islamic Prayer is so sacred that it is prohibited for one to eat, drink, or hold a conversation as they pray.

Muslims are commanded to pray in how was taught by Prophet Muhammad peace be upon him. The Islamic prayer movements comprise standing, bowing, and prostrating. According to our Prophet, man is closest to God when he is in prostration. The Prayer comprises recitations from the Holy Quran, praises of the Almighty, and supplications seeking guidance, forgiveness, and more.

"And establish Prayer and give Zakah and bow with those who bow [in worship and obedience]" (Quran 2:43)

While not mandated, it is highly encouraged for one to awaken in the middle of the night to pray to God, as this is a common practice of righteous people.

The Islamic Prayer is a ritual which has been unchanged for more than 1400 years and is repeated five times a day by hundreds of millions of people all around the globe. Earlier Prophets and Messengers also performed Salah prayer, in which the act of prostration was involved. According to the Gospel of Mathew, Prophet Jesus fell with his face to the ground and prayed: *'Going a little farther, he fell with his face to the ground and prayed: 'My Father, if it is possible, may this cup be taken from me. Not as I will, but as you will'"(Mathew 26:39)*

It's important to note that God is transcendent, free of all needs, and independent. He is in no need of human worship or reverence, as He gains nothing from it. Muslims do not pray or worship God for God's sake; instead, they praise and worship God for their own sake. God made worship and the remembrance of Him beneficial to mankind, both in this world and the next.

"And whoever strives only strives for [the benefit of] himself. Indeed, Allah is free from need of the worlds" (Quran 29:6)

The benefits of praying to the Almighty are vast, and the blessings of Prayer are beyond our imagination. Prayer motivates one to do good and strive for the best, so one can live a good life in this world--and in the next world, eternally.

"Indeed, I am Allah. There is no deity except Me, so worship Me and establish Prayer for My remembrance" (Quran 20:14)

ZAKAT
(GIVING ALMS TO THE POOR & NEEDY)

Zakat is the third pillar of Islam. *Zakat* in Arabic translates to *'the act of giving of alms to the poor and needy.'* Offering Zakat is a religious obligation for Muslims. In Islam, it is considered the duty of individuals with wealth to assist the poor and needy. The term Zakat in Arabic linguistically has several meanings, including 'to purify, to increase, cleanliness, blessings, and goodness.'

Zakat means to purify; because, according to the Islamic faith, one's wealth and property are not pure unless the owner shares a divinely appointed proportion with people in need. The principle of Zakat also purifies one's heart of greed and selfishness. Whereas the humanistic love of wealth is natural, Zakat is intended to free Muslims from the excessive and all-consuming love of money and selfish desire; teaching self-discipline.

"Take, [O, Muhammad], from their wealth a charity by which you purify them and cause them increase and invoke [Allah's blessings] upon them. Indeed, your invocations are reassurance for them. And Allah is Hearing and Knowing" (Quran 9:103)

Zakat also means growth and blessings; because if one were to give and help others in times of ease and difficulties, God will be pleased and return with increase and bless his wealth. Allah, the Glorious, has promised that the one who spends his wealth in Zakat will see his prosperity increased manifold.

"The example of those who spend their wealth in the way of Allah is like a seed [of grain] which grows seven spikes; in each spike is a

hundred grains. And Allah multiplies [His reward] for whom He wills. And Allah is all-Encompassing and Knowing" (Quran 2:261)

Our Prophet has stated that the act of Charity does not decrease wealth; instead, it blesses, purifies and ultimately increases one's fortune.

There are three primary types of giving in Islam. Two of these giving methods are mandatory, while one is highly recommended but not obligatory. The first obligatory act of giving is called *Zakat Al-Mal*, which is the Zakat given from one's saved wealth and liquid assets. The second obligatory Zakat is called *Zakat Al-Fitr*, which is a special Zakat due at the end of the Month of Ramadan—to be paid by the head of the household. The third type of giving in Islam is called *Sadaqah*, which is voluntary and can be given at any time on any amount.

Sadaqah comes from an Arabic word meaning sincerity, as giving Sadaqah or charity is a sign of sincere faith in God by the person who gives it. Sadaqah is described in the Holy Quran as a beautiful loan; which includes any act of charitable giving made as a gesture of love and generosity; whether the act stands in the form of giving money or time, helping others, praying for someone, spreading knowledge, giving advice, forgiving someone, visiting the sick, or even smiling at someone.

Zakat plays a significant role and holds a commendable high standard in Islam, to the extent that about three dozen Verses in the Holy Quran link the obligatory prayer to charity. God describes the true believers as the ones that both pray their obligatory prayers and give Zakat. This proves the concept that Zakat is the believer's most important obligation, after the obligatory prayer.

"Indeed, those who believe and do righteous deeds and establish Prayer and give Zakah will have their reward with their Lord, and there will be no fear concerning them, nor will they grieve" (Quran 2:277)

All things belong to God, and God has given wealth to specific individuals so they can distribute resources to those not as fortunate. People are given wealth as a trust from God, to distribute to and benefit the ones in need. The true Owner of all things is not man, but God, and we human beings are merely His trustees. God, the Glorious, who provided wealth to the intended recipient, reserved a portion of the resources for the poor, so the underprivileged have a right to claim a portion of one's wealth. The concept of Zakat reminds Muslims that everything they possess belongs to the Almighty.

People are given their wealth as a test from God. Wealth should be acquired, distributed, and spent in a way which is pleasing to God.

"And it is He who has made you successors upon the Earth and has raised some of you above others in degrees [of rank] that He may try you through what He has given you" (Quran 6:165)

The acquisition and hoarding of wealth for one's own sake to increase a man's worth, is condemned. Mere acquisition of wealth counts for nothing in the sight of the Almighty, as it does not give man any merit—in this life or the hereafter. Islam teaches that one should acquire wealth to spend it on his/her self, family, and people in need. The act of giving and helping others shows one's love of God, more than the amount or quantity of one's own wealth; as when they give to others, they donate funds they otherwise would have spent on themselves--doing so to please God the Almighty. Zakat is a sign of true belief and love in God.

"The ones who establish prayer, and from what We have provided them, they spend. Those are the believers, truly. For them are degrees [of high position] with their Lord and forgiveness and noble provision" (Quran 8:3-4)

Zakat offers both humanitarian and socio-political benefits. It is designed by our Creator to reallocate and redistribute wealth in a society. Zakat establishes social justice and—if practiced collectively by a population—can lead a community to prosperity and security. Zakat helps to circulate wealth in a balanced way, stabilizing and equalizing the flow of money in a society; eliminating as it does the eternal cycle of poverty. Zakat is an interest-free financial strategy that could help prevent society from undergoing an economic recession.

Every Muslim who has wealth exceeding a specific minimum—a level known as *Nisab*—and who maintains that wealth for over one lunar year, must give Zakat. Zakat is given annually based on the Islamic lunar calendar and is not based on the western calendar—which is 11 days longer than its counterpart.

The *Nisab* is the specific minimum amount of wealth that a Muslim must possess before being required to pay Zakat. One must pay Zakat if what they own is equal to or more than the equivalent to 3 ounces of gold, or its value in cash or trade goods. Zakat must be paid for gold and silver currency, cash, agricultural produce such as date farms, livestock, rent income, and business commodities such as inventory stock in a shop warehouse.

Islam requires Muslims to pay an annual contribution of 2.5 percent of the wealth and liquid assets they have accrued and held for over the course of one lunar year. Zakat is calculated on the person's earned net balance; that amount which remains after paying all other necessary expenses. Zakat is not an income tax, rather the amount due is based on what a Muslim has saved and held for an entire year, and not on their income level. Zakat is not paid from the pool of funds used for debt repayment, or necessary living expenses such as food, water, shelter, clothing, and transportation.

The recipients of Zakat are the poor, the needy individuals who live in turmoil, those who have accumulated much debt, captives, the Zakat administrators, and more recipients. Scholars state that the poor and the impoverished are the most important categories of people eligible to receive Zakat.

"Zakah expenditures are only for the poor and for the needy and for those employed to collect [Zakah] and for bringing hearts together [for Islam] and for freeing captives [or slaves] and for those in debt and for the cause of Allah and for the [stranded] traveler - an obligation [imposed] by Allah. And Allah is Knowing and Wise" (Quran 9:60)

The purpose of Zakat is to help those who cannot help themselves. Zakat can be given to an individual's extended family; however, one may not give this specified amount to his parents or his children, as one is already obligated to support them. When one offers Zakat in this world, he or she is really helping themselves; as they are transferring needed goodwill from their worldly life to their afterlife, which is the best investment one can make.

When one gives to someone in need, he shouldn't think of the gesture as a favor; instead, he is giving to God. The one giving is more in need of the beggar, than the beggar needs him. Whereas the beggar is in need only of money, the giver needs the Almighty's forgiveness.

> **"Do they not know that it is Allah who accepts repentance from His servants and receives charities and that it is Allah who is the Accepting of repentance, the Merciful?"**
> **(Quran 9:104)**

The benefits of giving in charity are many and varied. Amongst the benefits is the pleasure that God expresses to the one who gives. Zakat is known to extinguish the Wrath that the Almighty may hold for one who doesn't give. Giving Zakat also protects one from the punishment of hellfire. The act of giving to the needy awakens the soul and initiates genuine concern and sympathy for the well-being of the underprivileged and others.

It is recommended to give charity in secrecy to ensure that one is offering for the right, pure reason, of pleasing God, and not to receive praise or to boast before others—both acts which would nullify good deeds. However, under certain circumstances--for instance, if one has the intention to encourage others to donate similarly one may give Zakat in public.

It's important to note that Zakat money needs to be given from an untainted pool of 100% pure and halal funds—not taken from thefts or bribes, nor profits from interest-based loans or from sales of alcohol, pork, drugs, or anything that is prohibited in Islam. God, the Almighty is Good and Pure and only accepts that which is good and pure.

Fasting in the Holy Month of Ramadan

The Holy Month of Ramadan is the ninth month of the Islamic lunar calendar and can last 29 or 30 days. The Islamic calendar is based on a lunar year of 12 full lunar cycles, taking 354 or 355 days. The moon circles the Earth twelve times in a full lunar year. The observance of a new moon marks the beginning of each month. When a new moon is sighted, Ramadan begins and then fasting would commence in the next dawn. If a new moon is not sighted, then Muslims would start their fast the following day.

Islam is built upon five pillars and fasting during the Month of Ramadan is the 4th pillar of Islam. Muslims fast by abstaining from eating, drinking, chewing gum, smoking, and involving in any sexual activity from dawn to sunset. Fasting in Islam does not solely comprise refraining from food and drinks; instead one is to abstain from every kind of evil, selfish desire, and wrongdoing. The purpose of fasting is not merely for the body; instead, it's for the spirit as well. Fasting in Ramadan is for the soul, mind, and body. Muslims are commanded to refrain against gossiping, backbiting, slandering, lying, cheating, looking at what's prohibited, nursing a grudge, using sinful speech, and any wrongdoing. Muslims must adhere to the morals of Islam strictly during their fast as failure to do so can violate one's fast.

Fasting in Ramadan is obligatory for every sane, healthy Muslim, who is not ill or traveling long distance whether male or female unless a female is on her menstruation cycle or having post-childbirth bleeding. Most religions practice some fasting that generally requires one to go without food or drinks for a specified period. According to the Bible, Jesus fasted for 40 days.

… But why do Muslims Fast? The primary reason Muslims fast is because God the Almighty has commanded them to do so in His Last and Final Revelation, the Holy Quran. The Holy Quran was sent down to the last and final nation, our nation, whereas the Bible, Torah, and all previous scriptures were sent to former nations. God states in the Quran:

"O, you who believe! Fasting is prescribed to you as it was prescribed to those before you, that ye may become righteous and (hopefully learn) self-restraint" (Quran 2:183)

Fasting is an act of worship beloved by God. The Holy Month of Ramadan & the prescribed fasting is a gift and mercy to Muslims from the Almighty. God prescribes none rulings to his slaves unless there are great wisdom and benefit behind it.

… But How is Ramadan & Fasting a gift & mercy to the ones that fast sincerely? Sin is defined as an act of disobedience in which a person goes against the commandments of God. God deliberately placed human beings on Earth knowing they will sin. By nature of human beings, mankind is fallible and bound to sin due to outside evil influences whether it's from friends, family, the media, or from Satan's attack and whispers that can stray one from the straight path leading them to destruction. God is willing to accept anyone's repentance. It is, in fact, Allah that loves people who repent repeatedly. Since Muslims are erred to sin because of ignorance, forgetfulness, or from the handiwork of Satan. Mankind needs to be reminded and trained from abstaining from harmful behaviors that go against the commandments of God. God, the Almighty states fasting and abstaining from which is prohibited will increase one's *Taqwa*.

God the Almighty states fasting and abstaining from which is prohibited will increase one's Taqwa. Taqwa is translated to God-fearing piety, righteousness, mindfulness, and consciousness of God where one is aware God is watching at all times. The concept of Taqwa is expressed in the Holy Koran over 200 times. The word Taqwa comes from the root word 'to guard' When one has Taqwa or God consciousness, one loves to do good and avoid evil for the sake of God.

….But how does one attain Taqwa by fasting? Fasting is a shield for mankind. Fasting protects a person from sin and lustful desires. The purpose of fasting is not merely physical training to withstand hunger, thirst, and exhaustion; instead, it is disciplining the soul & the ego to give up what's loved in this world from material goods, wealth, etc. for the sake of God. Fasting Muslims seek to overpower and suppress sinful desires in themselves, putting aside all evils and bad behaviors to express their dedication and love to God and use it to draw closer to Him so that God becomes a reality in their lives resulting in a higher spiritual state. Fasting in Ramadan offers one to develop spiritually and gain strength and control over one's soul and one's ego which would dominate one's life when left unchecked and unmonitored.

Sincere and proper fasting for the full month of Ramadan every year is very beneficial for individuals and society as it develops piety and self-restraint.

Once one is conscious that God is watching, one's sins and disobedience will dramatically decrease. Fasting in Ramadan recharges one's spiritual and physical state. Fasting is meant to instill virtuous qualities in humans from being generous, patient, while cleansing the spiritual heart. Fasting cleansing the soul, mind, and body as temporally giving up food, water, and many disobedient acts is a natural way of removing toxins from the soul, mind, and body. When Fasting, one controls the urge to eat and drink empowering one to exercise self-control and help to develop patience, inner strength and will-power in a person.

Fasting develops good qualities of endurance and self-restraint, helping one control his or her anger, tongue, and actions. Fasting help resists unlawful desires and wicked habits which would help guard one against evil. Fasting in Ramadan suppresses worldly desires and strengthens one's spirituality.

The Holy Month of Ramadan is special and blessed because the Holy Quran, which is God's final Book, was revealed to Prophet Mohammad Peace Be Up Him, in this special month. Therefore, Muslims recite the Holy Qur'an frequently in this blessed month. Ramadan is the month when Muslims try to establish or re-establish a relationship with their Creator and the Holy Qur'an so that one may be guided. Ramadan is a month for deep inner reflection.

Muslim believe they earn extra spiritual rewards in this month for good deeds which can lead them to paradise in the hereafter and avoid the punishment of the hellfire. During Ramadan, Muslims engage in consistent spiritual reflection and prayer with the aims of drawing closer to God and becoming a better person.

During this blessed month, extra voluntary prayers are offered in every Mosque well into the night, with many places of worship crammed with worshippers. Hearts are directed away from worldly material goods and get directed to Almighty, His Religion, and His Final Revelation, the Holy Quran. Due to the blessings and rewards associated with this Holy Month, Muslims are encouraged to give and help others to the best of their ability. While the primary reason for fasting is to draw closer to Allah by purifying oneself by abstaining from sins and increasing acts of good, fasting comes with many additional benefits. Amongst the benefits of fasting is that it teaches man the principle of sincere Love to God as he struggles to fast solely for the pleasure of God.

Fasting in Ramadan is supposed to help discontinue any bad habits one may have developed throughout the year. Fasting is supposed to free a person from the slavery of sinful desires as they give it up for a whole month. Fasting develops new good habits as Muslims increase acts of good in this month.
Fasting in Ramadan is a way of experiencing hunger, thirst, exhaustion, and developing sympathy for the less fortunate which should cause an increase in helping the less fortunate. Many take blessings like food and water for granted. When one is fasting, he or she realizes what the less fortunate feel every day. This should increase helping and giving others, especially the less fortunate as fasting helps one to sympathize with the poor so one may know and experience their hardships.

Fasting in Ramadan leads one to be more thankful and appreciate all of God's gifts and provisions. Fasting is a way to humble one before God and His creation, as hunger and thirst help one come in a realization they desperately need God and his provisions decreasing one's false pride and arrogance. Fasting in Ramadan teaches patience as one feels the pains of deprivation, but he endures them patiently. Fasting teaches moderation and increases one will-power as one feels hunger but disciplines him or herself not to eat so they can benefit from the increased will-power and discipline after the month is over. This month is supposed to be a training period for the rest of the year so that one can be better equipped to resist temptations.

Amongst the many spiritual benefits, lie many physicality benefits. Fasting in Ramadan speeds up one's metabolism, lowers cholesterol levels, helps with weight loss, indorses longevity, improves one's brain function, clears one's skin from acne and dry skin, improves the immune system, and purifies the body by allowing the body to rest from the continuous task of digesting food.

Whereas fasting in the Month of Ramadan may appear very exhausting and challenging, it is, in fact, an enjoyable time for Muslims. It becomes a month of family and friends getting together to worship the One God and to eat together after sunset. Ramadan has a different atmosphere from other months of the year. Often, local families and individuals sponsor breaking-fast and dinners at local mosques open to the community. Mosques are often packed with worshippers at night and they usually hold special evening prayers in mosques during Ramadan.

After the month, Muslims celebrate one of the two Islamic festivals; *Eid-ul-Fitr* which translates to the *'festival of the breaking of the Fast'* It is a festival of celebration. It is a time of joy, a social gathering of family and friends, gift giving, wearing new clothes, and time which Muslims express thanks and gratitude to their Creator for the self-control, will, strength and the endurance and benefits they practiced and achieved during this Holy Month.

HAJJ
(PILGRIMAGE TO MECCA)

The fifth pillar of Islam is *Hajj*, which translates to mean *'the pilgrimage to the Holy city of Makkah'* The Arabic word Hajj, linguistically, means *'heading to a place for the sake of visiting'*; in Islamic terminology, it describes the act of heading to Makkah to observe specific acts and rituals. Hajj, or the pilgrimage, is a 5-6-day journey to this sacred place between the 8th and 13th day of the last month of the Islamic lunar calendar, Dhul-Hijjah. The Hajj journey is obligatory for every Muslim, male or female, to complete at least once in a lifetime; providing that they are mentally, physically and financially capable of making the trip. God states:

"...And [due] to Allah from the people is a pilgrimage to the House - for whoever is able to find thereto a way..." (Quran 3:97)

The Hajj includes detailed reenactments of certain symbolic rituals performed by great Prophets and righteous individuals in the past. The Hajj Pilgrimage and its symbolic rituals commemorate the legacy of Prophet Abraham peace be upon him, so one needs to learn about Prophet Abraham to understand the reasoning behind individual acts performed as a part of Hajj.

Integral to Hajj is the Kaaba, a Holy Shrine, a black silk-clad cube stone structure at the heart of the Grand Mosque in the modern-day city of Mecca, Saudi Arabia. The Kaaba is at the center of the Earth, built by Prophet Abraham and his son Ismael peace be upon them. Upon completion, God the Almighty Commanded Prophet Abraham to relay the Message amongst the people that they would be required to make a pilgrimage to this House. Prophet Abraham peace be upon him replied, '*O Allah, with no one here, how will they hear my Message?*' God then answered, '*Upon you is the proclamation, and upon me, is to see who responds.*' Prophet Abraham peace be upon him went on top of the Kaaba and also climbed Mount Safa and called out, '*O People, Allah has built a house for himself on this Earth, and he has legislated upon you to perform pilgrimage, so come and perform pilgrim to this house!*'

"And proclaim to the people the Hajj [pilgrimage]; they will come to you on foot and on every lean camel; they will come from every distant pass" (Quran 22:27)

By performing Hajj, Muslims are answering the command of Allah. Over 4000 years later, to this day, millions upon millions of Muslims continue to answer the call of Prophet Ibrahim peace be upon him from every corner of the globe. You find Muslims from Africa, Asia, Europe, Australia, and all over the world making this pilgrimage every year. It is the largest annual convention of faith on Earth, where Muslims gather to commemorate the rituals observed by Prophet Abraham and his son, Ishmael peace be upon them. Muslims celebrate the legacy of Prophet Ibrahim and the many sacrifices he has made for the sake of God.

When Muslims enter the scared Makkan territory during Hajj, they bathe themselves and enter a ritually purified state called *Ahram*. In this state, pilgrims are forbidden to perform typical actions that are otherwise permissible, such as covering one's head for males, clipping their fingernails, cutting their hair, hunting animals, picking plants, engaging in sexual activity, and wearing traditional clothing for men.

Male Pilgrims wear two white seamless lyon sheets with no stitching by hand, that are wrapped around the body. No belts, no rings, no perfumes, no jewelry, or any accessories or garish clothing, may be worn. The simple garb worn represents complete impoverishment and humility and signifies the equality of humanity—as everyone comes before God the same. No one is better than the other among the pilgrims of Hajj. Muslims are all united in their devotion to God. Every human being is displayed equally, as we are all equal in the eyes of Allah regardless of our color or race. The black man stands next to the white man, and they call on Allah with one voice. The King stands beside a peasant; the businessman stands beside the politician, the doctor beside the engineer, and they declare their submission to the will of Allah using the same words. Several Millions of people are dressed the same way and look the same; no one can tell the rich from the poor; all fulfill the same rituals with the utmost humility. This is to remind pilgrims of the coming Day of Judgment when all people will be stripped of their clothes and displayed before their God. The pilgrims show a sense of poverty with their appearance, as the pilgrims acknowledge that they are the ones in need, and God is the one that owns and has everything they require.

Pilgrims start to perform their tawaf from the black stone corner. Tawaf is the act of circulating the Kaaba counterclockwise. Pilgrims circumambulate the Kaaba seven times while they recite prayers during each circuit. Pilgrims perform the tawaf (circumambulation) to follow the suit of the Prophet (peace be upon him) as has been ordained in the Qur'an. As Pilgrims circulate the Kaaba, they disconnect themselves from worldly attachments and focus upon the presence of the Divine. As Pilgrims circumambulate the Kabah, they chant: *'Here I am, O Allah, Here I am, you have no partner; indeed, all praise, favor, and dominion belong to you, you have no partner.'*

Since Prophet Abraham and his wife Sara could not bear any children, Sara asked her husband to marry their servant so they could beget a child before they were too old to raise offspring. Later, Prophet Abraham was commanded by God to take both his second wife Hagar and their son Ismael and leave them in a barren desert valley in modern-day Mecca. As soon as Prophet Abraham peace be upon him started to leave, Hagar cried out, *'Where are you going? Why are you leaving us?'* Abraham did not respond. After a few more attempts to find answers, Hagar then asked if this action was a commandment from God. He responded, *'Yes.'* Then she replied, *'if God commanded you to leave us, then leave us, because God never will leave us to perish."* She was sure that God would not abandon her and her child, despite their presence at the center of a Desert Valley. He left them with little water and some dates.

Later, Hagar ran out of food and water and started to worry for her child. She then fell into a state of anxiety and climbed a hillock called Mount Safa, crying out, *'is anyone there?'* Then she ran to another hillock—Mount Marwa—again crying out, *'Is anyone there?'* Then she paced back and forth to each mountain, seven times.

On the seventh round, Hajar saw Angel Gabriel descend from the sky and strike the ground with his wing, causing water to gush upward from the Earth. Angel Gabriel declared, *'Zam, Zam,'* meaning *'Stop, Stop,'* commanding the water to stop. This water is now referred to as *Zam Zam Water*. This well to this today nourishes pilgrims of Mecca every day.

Passersby rescued Hagar and her child. Years later, when Ismael was growing to become a man, his father Prophet Abraham returned and built with him the house in Mecca, called the Kabah.

In commemoration of this great sacrifice from Hagar, Muslim pilgrims in Hajj progress in a quicker pace going back and forth between the two hillocks (which are 300-400 yards apart) seven times, reenacting Hagar's movements when attempting to find aid. This action is symbolic of Hagar's search for water and the miracle of the well of Zam Zam.

Then the pilgrims depart Mecca toward the valley of Minna, which is about 3-4 miles outside of Makkah. During Hajj season, Minna is full of over 100,000 air-conditioned tents that cover every open space as far as the eye can see, row after row, where pilgrims stay overnight. The tents accommodate roughly 2-3 million people performing Hajj. Pilgrims spend their time in prayer, worship, and meditation, asking for forgiveness on the night known as *Layali Al-Tashreeq*.

After spending the night at the village of Mina, pilgrims take the next step and proceed to a large plain about 7-8 miles from Mecca called *Arafat*, a large plain surrounded by bare mountains. Forming the center is a hill known as *Mount Mercy (Gabal Al-Rahma)*, where Prophet Muhammad peace be upon him delivered his memorable Farewell Sermon. This is the central rite of the entire Hajj. Pilgrims stand from noon to sunset praying quietly before God, begging for mercy and forgiveness and asking their wishes. Many pilgrims shed tears as they ask the Al-Mighty to forgive them their sins in this very emotional day of standing. Standing, reflecting, considering their actions, and begging and pleading to God is often thought of as a preview and representation of the great assembly of the upcoming Day of Judgment. It is to remind people of the fateful day where everyone will stand before their Lord begging for mercy.

Then pilgrims spend the night at Muzdalifah, an open plain about halfway between Arafat and Mina where pilgrims pray, then go back to Mina.

At 95, Prophet Abraham peace be upon him saw himself slaughtering his son in a dream; interpreting the vision to mean that he needed to slaughter his son for the sake of God. He was to lay his son on to the sand and raise a knife to sacrifice him. Islam doesn't allow this act; the dream was only a way for God to test Prophet Abraham. But Prophet Abraham didn't know that this was only a test to see who he loved and was devoted to the most; his Lord or his son. Ismael was his only progeny at the time. His son looked at his father and said, *'if God commanded you to do this, do as you were commanded as I too am submissive to God.'*

As Prophet Abraham peace be upon him raised his sword, Satan appeared in front of him and stated, *'that's your only son, what are you doing? How can you kill him?'* Prophet Abraham, recognizing Satan the cursed, started to pelt him with seven stones until he went away. After that, Prophet Abraham moved to another place, where Satan once again returned and was pelted again by Prophet Abraham; then again, the action was repeated in another place. Satan always tries to separate people from their Lord. Eventually, when Prophet Abraham was poised to kill his son, his son was replaced with a Ram sent down by God. Prophet Abraham immediately realized that this was only a test from the Almighty.

At Minna, pilgrims take part in a ritual known as the *ramy*, which is the throwing of seven stones at three monuments called *Al-Jamarāt*. Until today, millions of Muslims pass by three monuments and throw pebbles as a ritual, which symbolizes the reenactment of the actions of Prophet Ibrahim when he faced the trial of sacrificing his son. The three monuments or pillars in Mina represent the three places that the Devil tempted Prophet Abraham to forego the sacrifice. The throwing of the pebbles is purely symbolic. To this day, at the end of Hajj, Muslims annually sacrifice sheep, cows, camels, and goats in the millions; commemorating the spirit of Prophet Abraham peace be upon him, his intention, his sincerity, and his passion. The meat from the sacrifice is then given to the needy.

During Hajj, Muslims also kiss a black stone, symbolizing their apperception of being invited to the house of the King of all Kings— our Lord, our Creator. Muslims also kiss the black stone in tradition of Prophet Muhammad peace be upon him. If they cannot kiss it, they can touch it or point in its direction. This stone was sent down from Heaven for Prophet Abraham peace be upon him, to be used for the construction of the sacred house. Buildings in ancient times often had cornerstones, and Prophet Abraham wanted a cornerstone for this house. Narrations describe the stone as being whiter than milk darkening slowly from the sins of humans until it morphed into a black stone. The black stone is the starting-point for tawaf — the circling of the Kabah.

Hajj is completed by the act of men either shaving their heads or clipping their hair, and women cutting off a fingertip's length of their hair, to mark their partial deconsecration; a symbol of humility.

Apart from Hajj, a minor pilgrimage known as *Umrah* is performed in the year's remainder. The completion of Umrah does not fulfill the obligation of Hajj. Umrah is much shorter, lasting a few hours which entail the seven circumambulations of the Kabah and the light jogging between Mount Safa and Mount Mara.

This spiritual journey known as Hajj boasts many benefits, including a powerful positive transformation that makes pilgrims more spiritual, righteous, softer, and better human beings overall. Pilgrims who embark on the journey of Hajj faithfully and sincerely are cleansed of all their previous sins, leaving them with a fresh start.

Upon completion of Hajj, Muslims celebrate one of two Muslim Holidays called *Eid Al-Adha*. Muslims celebrate by praying to God and visiting family and friends to thank and praise God for all the blessings He has bestowed upon them.

SHIRK IN ISLAM

The word Shirk comes from an Arabic word generally meaning, *'to share.'* In the context of Religion, it means giving Rights of Allah to someone other than Allah (God). Shirk is the act of ascribing a partner or rival to Allah in Lordship (Ruboobiyyah).

Only God has the right to be worshipped or venerated. One who believes that anyone other than Allah created him or believes there is an entity worthy of worship besides Allah (God), is committing the grave sin of *Shirk*. Shirk is often translated to mean the practice of *polytheism*. The act of Shirk includes failing to worship God, denying His Existence, and sharing or associating a partner with Him; whether the partner is a prophet, an idol, the sun, the moon, or any other being or thing.

Shirk is considered the most severe sin in Islam. Shirk is regarded as the cardinal sin in Islam. Shirk nullifies all of one's good deeds and denies one the rewards of the hereafter.

"And it was already revealed to you and those before you that if you should associate [anything] with Allah, your work would surely become worthless, and you would surely be among the losers" (Quran 39:65)

Shirk is the only sin that God will not forgive of an individual, if not sincerely repented for before his or her death.

"Indeed, Allah does not forgive association with Him, but He forgives what is less than that for whom He wills. And he who associates others with Allah has certainly fabricated a tremendous sin" (Quran 4:48)

If one repents and ceases from engaging in Shirk, then he or she would be forgiven; as repentance wipes out every sin, without exception, as long as one repents before death.

The very reason for our creation was to worship the One God solely, and not anyone or anything else. Shirk denies the purpose of man's creation. Shirk deviates from the natural state of man, which is the belief in the One God and the worship of Him Alone. It was not until much later that Shirk started to spread in humanity—after the existence of *Tawheed (monotheism- the worship of the One God)*.

Worshipping and praising deities other than Allah, who have no power to benefit or harm, is an act of injustice to Allah—who created this whole Universe and gave life to you and me. Shirk is also an act of ingratitude. Shirk is the root of evil and causes the greatest downfall of human dignity and status.

Islam strictly states that all types of prayers should only be directed to God the Almighty, and no one or nothing else. God is in total control of every man's destiny and is the only One that can benefit a person, grant one's needs and desires, and that can remove one's harm and distress.

In the Holy Qur'an, one that engages in Shirk is referred to as a *'mushrik'* or *'mushrikeen'* (in its plural form) --- one that takes part in Shirk and plots against Islam. The Holy Quran refers to them as the enemies of Islam.

The mainstream Christian belief of the Trinity is considered a type of Shirk, although not the worst kind of Shirk, such as worshipping, bowing down, or sacrificing for an idol or an image. Any shared divinity is considered Shirk.

"They have certainly disbelieved who say, 'Allah is the third of three,' And there is no god except one God. And if they do not desist from what they are saying, there will surely afflict the disbelievers among them a painful punishment" (Quran 5:73)

The opposite of Shirk is *Tawheed (Monotheism),* which is the maintaining and observing of the worship of the One and True Creator while acknowledging his Uniqueness and Attributes. The Christian belief that Jesus is the son of God, or God himself, is the direct opposite of Tawheed.

"They have certainly disbelieved who say that Allah is Christ, the son of Mary..."
(Quran 5:17)

Trinity—father, son, holy spirit—and the concept that Jesus died for our sins is firmly rejected in Islam.

"O People of the Scripture, do not commit excess in your Religion or say about Allah except the Truth. The Messiah, Jesus, the son of Mary, was but a messenger of Allah and His word which He directed to Mary and a soul [created at a command] from Him. So, believe in Allah and His messengers. And do not say, 'Three'; desist - it is better for you. Indeed, Allah is but one God. Exalted is He above having a son. To Him belongs whatever is in the Heavens and whatever is on the Earth. And sufficient is Allah as Disposer of affairs"
(Quran 4:171)

God makes it clear in the Koran that the act of ascribing a son to Him, angers him. Ascribing a son to God is beneath the Almighty. God states:

"And they say: 'The Most Beneficent (Allah) has begotten a son (or offspring or children) Indeed you have brought forth (said) a terrible evil thing. Whereby the Heavens are almost torn, and the Earth is split asunder, and the mountains fall in ruins. That they ascribe a son (or offspring or children) to the Most Beneficent (Allah). But it is not suitable for (the Majesty of) the Most Beneficent that He should beget a son" (Quran 88-92)

Having multiple gods is illogical. According to the Holy Quran, there can only be One God; if there were various gods, they would have been competing to establish superior strength. The aggressive presence of two gods would have also destroyed the Heavens and the Earth.

"If there were in the Heavens and the Earth other gods besides Allah, there would be confusions in both (Heaven and Earth), but glory be to Allah, the Lord of, the throne; high is He above what they attribute to Him" (Quran 21:22)

Shirk is a very serious matter in Religion, as it makes something scared that God has not made sacred—an act of obscuring the truth. The Holy Koran and Sunnah (sayings of Prophet Muhammad peace be upon him) indicate that the act of Shirk sometimes expels a person from the Religion of Islam, and sometimes it does not. Therefore, Islamic scholars divided Shirk into the categories of *Major Shirk (Shirk Al-Akbar)* and *Minor Shirk (shirk Al-Asghar)*.

Major Shirk (Shirk Al-Akbar) is very serious and takes one out of the folds of Islam. Major Shirk is ascribing to someone other than Allah something that belongs Only to Allah, the Glorious, such as Lordship (ruboobiyyah), Divinity (uloohiyyah), and the Divine Names and Attributes of God (Al-Asma' Wa-sifaat). These 'gods' can be in the form of priests, kings, objects, animals, spirits, or anyone or anything other than Allah, the Almighty.

Major Shirk can come in the form of beliefs, words, or actions. Major Shirk can be seen outwardly, such as when one worships idols or graves; and can be hidden, such as when one who relies upon gods other than Allah.

Major Shirk occurs when one prays or supplicates to one other than Allah. Major Shirk includes believing someone or something other than Allah who creates and gives life and death and is in full control of everything. Major Shirk also comprises the belief that someone other than Allah must be obeyed. Major Shirk also includes the idea that others apart from Allah know the unseen. Major Shirk also comprises the act of loving something that is a created being, equally or more than Allah. For example, this occurs when one is so emotionally attached to wealth, they make its attainment their goal in life. Wealth becomes everything to them. Those individuals took money as their God.

Major Shirk also includes loving to obey one's desires more than Allah. One would follow their desires even if it leads to disobeying Allah. Such one takes their desires as their god as they act according to their whims. God states:

"Have you seen he who has taken as his god his [own] desire, and Allah has sent him astray due to knowledge and has set a seal upon his hearing and his heart and put over his vision a veil? So, who will guide him after Allah? Then will you not be reminded?" (Quran 45:23)

Minor Shirk (Shirk Al-Asghar) does not make the doer a disbeliever or remove one from the folds of Islam. However, minor Shirk is still a major sin. Minor Shirk includes everything that may lead to major Shirk. Minor Shirk consists of any action which is done to gain praise, fame or any other worldly purpose. This is considered Shirk because the individual is doing an action for other people, instead of for the sake of God. Examples of this can take the form of praying to God in front of others, intending to gain praise from people, or the case of donating to a charity to show off, to gain fame, or for any worldly purpose. When one commits such action, the good action gets nullified, and the doer receives no reward for it. Our Prophet stated: *'The thing I fear most for you is minor Shirk.' They (the Companions) said, 'O Messenger of Allah, what is Minor Shirk?' He (peace be upon him) said, 'Riya.' Indeed, Allah (Blessed and Exalted be He) shall say on the Day of Resurrection to the people who used to do good deeds for show: Go to those for whom you were showing off with your acts in worldly life and see if you can find with them recompense.'*

Minor Shirk also includes swearing oaths made by those other than Allah; for example, saying, *'I swear by such as such...'* It can be major Shirk depending on particular situations. Minor Shirk also includes the belief in evil omens or superstitions.

When the act of minor Shirk becomes a habit in all of one's deeds, it becomes Major Shirk.

One should be cautious of Shirk, as this evil can be inconspicuous and not as noticeable. Our Prophet stated: *'Ash-Shirk-al-Khafi (The inconspicuous Shirk) in the Muslim nation is more inconspicuous than the creeping of a black ant on a black rock in the pitch-darkness of the night.'* Therefore, one should take extra precaution to avoid the commission of this sin.

According to the Holy Qur'an, one who commits Shirk and believes in a deity other than Allah— will live a life of constant fear and anxiety.

"We will cast terror into the hearts of those who disbelieve for what they have associated with Allah of which He had not sent down [any] authority. And their refuge will be the Fire, and wretched is the residence of the wrongdoers" (Quran 3:151)

JIHAD IN ISLAM

Islam is generally misunderstood, especially in the western world, and no Islamic term is more widely misunderstood and evokes such strong reactions as the word *Jihad*. Jihad is often mistranslated to mean *'Holy War,'* and some non-Muslims misunderstand the term to mean waging war against disbelievers to either convert them to Islam or to kill them. Often the word Jihad is thought to be synonymous with terrorism. In reality, this couldn't be further from the truth.

Jihad comes from an Arabic word meaning to *'make an effort'* or *'to strive towards a goal.'* The term Jihad means to *'to exert oneself'* or *'to struggle.'* In the Islamic context, it means to struggle against one's evil inclination. So, any effort of self-improvement, whether in the form of improving One's spirituality, education, or financial situation, is an act of Jihad. The Holy Quran makes it clear that Jihad has been used to mean *'striving'* or *'exerting.'*

"We shall certainly guide those who strive for Our cause to Our path. God is certainly with the righteous ones" (Quran 29:69)

This Verse applies to ones that spiritually struggle to attain closeness to and seek the pleasure of God.

Jihad comes in different forms. The most essential type of Jihad, which can be labeled as Major Jihad, is *Jihad An-Nafs (The Jihad of the soul)*. This is the spiritual struggle between the two powers within human beings; the soul and the body. The soul is prone to becoming corrupted, with the corruption arising from within oneself, from external influences, or both.

"Verily, the soul is inclined to evil" (Quran 12:53)

Islam expresses the importance of one to purify, to cleanse, and to restrain themselves from submitting to their sinful desires. They are expected to avoid acts of disobedience and are expected to perform acts of obedience which are pleasing to God. Islam expects its followers to give preference to their soul and their conscience over their body and desires, by striving to resist their urges and inner temptations.

"And whoever strives only strives for [the benefit of] himself. Indeed, Allah is free from need of the worlds" (Quran 29:6)

Islam places a great deal of emphasis on self-improvement, self-development, self-restraint, and self-control, shaping one's life in the best manner for one's benefit and the benefit of society at large. This Jihad is intended to purify the soul and involves struggling against the greed for worldly purposes, arrogance, pride, envy, jealousy, hatred, hypocrisy, insincerity, vanity, narcissism, and other evil traits which Satan uses to lead humanity astray into destruction. It is imperative for every Muslim to struggle and strive daily to overcome these evils to the best of their ability. The Jihad of the soul also includes the struggle to perform good deeds for the sake of God, to please Him and become closer to him. Allah states in His Book:

"He has succeeded who purifies it" (Quran 91:9)

Scholars state that the successors this Verse is referring to are those individuals that engage in purifying their souls by obeying God and restraining from sins and evil doing.

The other major type of Jihad is *Jihad Al-Shaytan (Jihad against Satan)*. Satan's main aim is to destroy the Religion of mankind by attacking them with continuous whispers regarding their belief in God and when in worship to tempt, corrupt and mislead people away from God's guidance.

"O, you who have believed, enter into submission completely [and perfectly] and do not follow the footsteps of Satan. Indeed, he is to you a clear enemy" (Quran 2:208)

The whispers of Satan can come to pious and righteous people and to wicked and evil individuals. These whispers can be detrimental to one's spiritual, emotional, physical, and psychological well-being, so it's essential for one to strive to fight against Satan; to ward off doubts that Satan stirs up that undermines one's faith in God and to ward off corrupt desires which he provokes.

These two types of Jihad are the foundation for all other varieties of Jihad and are obligatory upon everyone accountable. If one does not engage in these types of Jihad, he or she cannot venture into the other realm of Jihad, which involves battles against external enemies.

This introduces us to the other variety of Jihad: *the armed struggle against those who plot against Muslims*, which can be classified as Minor Jihad. When Muslims or their faith or territory is threatened under attack, Muslims are permitted to defend themselves. This Jihad is the act of striving in the battlefield, to fight in self-defense to protect one's own life, family, faith, wealth, and property. It also includes fighting against evil, operation, and tyranny to defend what is right and to combat oppression. This Jihad is the effort and struggles to improve society.

As stated earlier, Jihad does not mean Holy War. The Arabic word for Holy War is 'Harbun Muqaddasah.' The word Jihad does not imply Holy War, and the words 'Holy War' do not exist at all in the Holy Qur'an or any authentic Hadith (Sayings of Prophet Muhammad). The killing of innocent people—whether Muslim or non-Muslim—is condemned in Islam and is considered a major sin. Islam does not permit Muslims to fight against non-Muslims, solely based on their faith.

Islam is a religion of peace, mercy, and forgiveness. No one can be compelled to accept Islam.

"There shall be no compulsion in [acceptance of] the Religion. The right course has become clear from the wrong. So, whoever disbelieves in false deities and believes in Allah has grasped the most trustworthy handhold with no break in it. And Allah is Hearing and Knowing"
(Quran 2:256)

Muslims must convey and establish the proofs and evidence of Islam to people so that they can be differentiated from falsehood. Islam is clear in terms of its Message and Mission, both of which no one is compelled to accept. Whoever is not stubborn or arrogant in their acceptance will enter and accept Islam, and whoever rejects the Truth may do so. No one can threaten or harm anyone because they choose not to accept Islam. If one is compelled to accept this faith, then he/she is not a true Muslim at heart.

Islam does not allow for the fighting of noncombatants. Military conflicts are to be directed against only fighting soldiers, and not against innocent civilians. The acts such as those committed on 9/11 in the United States, for example, are classified as a major sin in Islam and carry the death penalty.

> **"...Whoever kills a soul unless for a soul or corruption [done] in the land – it is as if he had slain mankind entirely. And whoever saves one – it is as if he had saved mankind entirely..." (Quran 5:32)**

It is also forbidden for one to harm or kill oneself by any means. Suicide is a severe sin in Islam, a state of disbelief, and a loss of faith that is condemned by the Quran.

> **"... do not throw [yourselves] with your [own] hands into destruction. And do good; indeed, Allah loves the doers of good" (Quran 2:195)**

Unfortunately, there is a category of brainwashed Muslim youth who get drafted into misguided terrorist groups, who believe that upon exploding themselves that they would die as martyrs and get sent directly to Paradise. Islam condemns quite the contrary, suicide in any form.

If attacked, one is permitted to fight back in self-defense. Muslims should be keen to defend themselves and preserve their own lives.

> **"Permission [to fight] has been given to those who are being fought because they were wronged. And indeed, Allah is competent to give them victory" (22:39)**

However, if the other party refrains from aggression and offers peace, then Muslims are expected to extend their hand for peace in return.

"And if they incline to peace, then incline to it [also] and rely upon Allah. Indeed, it is He who is the Hearing, the Knowing" (Quran 8:61)

The first battle fought by our Prophet and his followers, called the *Battle of Badr,* was an act of defense against a group who plotted and waged war against the Muslims. When fighting in defense, the Holy Koran warns Muslims not to exceed their military actions beyond the proper limits.

"Fight in the way of Allah those who fight you but do not transgress. Indeed. Allah does not like transgressors" (Quran 2:190)

This type of fighting is permitted, as it is a lesser evil designed to rid the world of a bigger evil. It is committed with the purpose of enjoining the right and forbidding the wrong. It constitutes the act of fighting to defend Islam, rather than to spread it.

Islam has provided guidelines for fighting against the enemy in self-defense. Islam prohibits the killing of children, women, the elderly, the sick, monks in monasteries, rabbis, those who are sitting in places of worship, and the murder of any other noncombatant--even in a state of war and fighting. Islam does not allow torture of prisoners of war, mutilation, treason, rape, cutting down fruitful trees, or the destroying of cultivated fields or gardens, or the destruction of property. Islam also does not allow the slaughter of cows, sheep, and camels, except for food. Muslims are also forbidden from attacking wounded soldiers unless the wounded soldier is still fighting you. Islam only allows fighting with minimum necessary force.

Some enemies of Islam take the text of the Holy Quran and Hadith out of context, claiming Islam promotes violence and terrorism; even though Jihad has nothing to do with harming oneself or society. Jihad remains a noble matter; a noble strike for the sake of God.

HELLFIRE
ACCORDING TO ISLAM

L ife is a test, and the test ends upon death. Every little atom of good and evil one performs in his or her lifetime is recorded in their book of deeds which will be presented to them on the Day of Judgement and every soul will be held accountable for their actions. When one dies, he or she will remain in the grave waiting to be resurrected. While in the grave, the deceased souls that deserve to go to Hell will experience some suffering in the grave whereas the deceased souls that are bound for Paradise will experience peace while they wait for the Day of resurrection.

When the hour comes, God will raise every dead person including the Jinn (supernatural creatures) to judge them according to their deeds. God is The Judge, The Arbitrator who will Judge, recompense, reward and punish his creation. Whereas God is Most-Forgiving, he is also Just. If one's good deeds outweigh his bad deeds, he will enter Paradise and be amongst the successful. As for the one that his bad deeds outweigh his good deeds, he will enter the Hellfire. One of the most fundamental aspects of Islam is the purpose of life is to save oneself from the punishment of the Hell Fire and to enter Paradise eternally.

"Every soul will taste death, and you will only be given your [full] compensation on the Day of Resurrection. So he who is drawn away from the Fire and admitted to Paradise has attained [his desire]. And what is the life of this world except for the enjoyment of delusion"
(Quran 3:185)

Believing and accepting the reality of the Last Day, Judgement Day, Paradise and the Hellfire is a component of the six pillars of Iman (Faith) in which every Muslim must believe and accept to become a Muslim. There are many references to the Hell Fire throughout the Holy Quran.

The ones in the Hell Fire will suffer tremendously both physically and spiritually. The pain, the horrors, the anguish, the hardship, the humiliation, the restlessness, and all forms of punishments of the Hellfire cannot be imagined nor perceived, nor grasped by the human finite mind. Not everyone in the hell Fire will suffer the same. The gravity of one's sin will distinguish the severity of one's suffering.

Allah the exalted prepares the Hell Fire for those who do not believe in Him, believe in Gods other than Allah, rebel against God's Religion and Laws, and reject God's Message and Messengers. The Hellfire is also prepared for sinners, criminals, murders, tyrants, hypocrites, the proud and arrogant, the stubborn, and the unjust, and all forms of evil people.

"Do they not know that whoever opposes Allah and His Messenger - that for him is the Fire of Hell, wherein he will abide eternally? That is the great disgrace" (Quran 9:63)

Islam states one's salvation is based one's faith in Allah, His Messenger, good deeds, and God's Mercy. As part of the Justice of God the Almighty, He punishes no one or any group of people until He has sent them a Messenger relaying his Message and warning the people. It is the nature of God that he treats no one unjustly or unfairly.

"...And never would We punish until We sent a messenger" (Quran 17:15)

Of the biggest suffering the unbelievers and the evildoers will face is when they come into the realization on the Day of Judgment that they did not follow God's Message nor His Guidance and have failed, thus earning God's Wrath. Many of the dwellers of the Hellfire will instantly regret the choices they made in their lives and will beg for another chance. The Quran states:

And those who followed would say: 'If only We had one more chance, we would clear ourselves of them, as they have cleared themselves of us.' Thus, will Allah show them (The fruits of) their deeds as (nothing but) regrets. Nor will there be a way for them out of the Fire" (Quran 2:167)

The Quran shares a dialogue that will take place between the dwellers of the Hellfire and the Angel Gate Keeper of the Hell.

"It almost explodes in rage. Whenever a group is thrown into it, its keepers will ask them, 'Did there not come to you a warner?' They will reply: 'Yes indeed; a Warner did come to us, but we rejected him and said, 'Allah never sent down any (Message): You are but lost in a great delusion!' 'And they will add: 'Had we but listened [to those warnings], or [at least] used our own reason, we would not [now] be among those who are destined for the blazing flame!' They will then confess their sins: but far will be (Forgiveness) from the Companions of the Blazing Fire!" (Quran 67:8-10)

However, no matter how much the sinners beg for forgiveness, it would be too late. The intensity of the Fire will be so terrifying that people will disown their closest and most beloved people in their lives on the Day of Judgement and flee from them on this great Day.

"But when there comes the Deafening Blast. On the Day a man will flee from his brother. And his mother and his father. And his wife and his children. For every man, that Day, will be a matter adequate for him" (Quran 33-37)

Man will give up everything he holds dearest to him to save himself from the Hellfire.

They will be shown each other. The criminal will wish that he could be ransomed from the punishment of that Day by his children. And his wife and his brother. And his nearest kindred who shelter him. And whoever is on Earth entirely [so] then it could save him" (Quran 70:14)

A quick dip in the Hellfire will have a person forgetting about all the pleasures he or she had in their lifetime. Our Prophet narrated: *'One of the people of Hell who found the most pleasure in the life of this world will be brought forth on the Day of Resurrection and will be dipped into the Fire of Hell. Then he will be asked, 'O son of Adam, have you ever seen anything good?' Have you ever enjoyed any pleasure?' He will say, 'No, by God, O Lord.'*

Whereas there are a minority of scholars that state the Hell Fire is not eternal, most Islamic scholars' state that the polytheist and unbelievers will reside in the Hell Fire forever and that the Hell Fire is eternal for most people that enter it.

"Indeed, Allah has cursed the disbelievers and prepared for them a Blaze. Abiding therein forever, they will not find a protector or a helper" (Quran 33:64-65)

God, the Almighty created the Hell Fire and Paradise before mankind. Hell is so deep that if one were to drop a stone into it, it would take seventy years for that stone to hit its bottom. The Hellfire is black and dark as night.

The Hell Fire has various levels of severity and punishment according to the extent of disbelief and sins of those being punished in it. The lower the level of the Fire, the greater the intensity and punishment one suffers. Our Prophet narrated the lightest punishment of the Hellfire will be a man under the arch of whose feet will be placed a smoldering ember, and his brains will boil because of it. As for the most severe punishment in the Hellfire, it will go to the hypocrites, as God states in His Book:

"Indeed, the hypocrites will be in the lowest depths of the Fire - and never will you find for them a helper" (Quran 4:145)

The Hell Fire has Seven Gates in which its inhabitants will enter. Each gate deals with a specific group or category of sinners and each gate contain different torture and punishments. The distance between each gate is equal to the length of seventy years. Before the inhabitants of Hell enter, they will stand before the gate feeling the heat in terror. They will be shoved and piled thru the first gate until it fills, then the rest will be stacked and shoved into the second gate until it fills, and so on.

The Hell Fire has nineteen Angels who are led by the Chief Keeper of the Hellfire named *Angel Malik* who has never smiled since he was created. Angel Malik and the Angels of the Hellfire are very severe, harsh, and stern who would never disobey God's commandments.

After the inhabitants of the Hellfire enter, its gates will be shut and there will be no hope of escape for the dwellers of the Hellfire. The dwellers of the Hellfire will beg and plea to Angel Malik to let them out and he will respond 'Be quiet, surely, you shall abide forever!' The Angels of the Hellfire will have wipes made of iron which will whip the inhabitants in it. The dwellers of Hellfire will bear animosity and hate amongst other inhabitants of the Hellfire.

> **"Indeed, the criminals will be in the punishment of Hell, abiding eternally. (The torment) will not be lightened for them, and they will be plunged into destruction with deep regrets, sorrows and in despair therein. And We did not wrong them, but it was they who were the wrongdoers. And they will call, 'O Malik, let your Lord put an end to us!' He will say, 'Indeed, you will remain. We had certainly brought you the truth, but most of you, to the truth, were averse.' (Quran 43:-74-78)**

As for the Believers who practiced Tawheed (monotheism) and believed in the Prophet that was sent to them from God but lived a sinful life, they will be his punished in the Hell Fire for a length that commensurate the level of their sins. Then they would be brought out of it and eventually sent to Paradise. Some of them will be taken out of the Hell Fire with the intercession of their Prophets, some by the intercession of righteous individuals, and some will be taken out solely by the Mercy of God, the Most Merciful.

The Hell Fire has different names with different descriptions that are mentioned in the Islamic tradition. Amongst the names of the Hell Fire are:

Jaheem because of its blazing Fire
Jahannam because of the depth of its pit

Laẓā because of its blazing flames

Sa'eer because it is kindled and ignited

Saqar because of the intensity of its heat

Hatamah because it breaks and crushes anything into debris that is thrown into it

Haawiyah because whoever is thrown into it, is thrown from the top to the deep bottom of its chasm or abyss.

The dwellers of the Hellfire will be made huge, so every part of their body can feel the punishment. A person's molar tooth will be as big as Mount Uhud (a Mountain in the city of Medina). The distance between the shoulders of the dwellers of Hell will be equivalent to three days of walking.

The Fire that exists and burns in this world we live in is 1/70th of the severity and intensity of the Hellfire in the Hereafter. The Fire kindled by the Almighty will burn the skin of its inhabitants and every time their skin gets roasted; their skin will melt to their feet and God the Almighty will replace their burnt skin with a new one to be burnt again and the process will keep on repeating so they may taste the punishment. Other forms of punishment include super-heated scalding burring oil which will be poured on their heads in which will melt away and liquefy their internal organs. The inhabitants of the Hellfire will be in chains and shackles which will be tied around their necks and feet.

"Indeed, We have prepared for the disbelievers chains and shackles and a blaze" (Quran 76:4)

The clothing in the Hellfire will be garments of Fire tailored for them with copper so they will boil inside.

And you will see the criminals that Day bound together in shackles, their garments of liquid pitch and their faces covered by the Fire" (Quran 14:49-50)

The Quran references three types of food in the Hellfire which in fact worsen a sinner's torment when consumed. The food and drink of the Hellfire do not provide nourishment, nor does it relieve hunger nor thirst. The dwellers of the Hellfire will experience intense thirst only to have hot boiling water mixed with puss given to them. Water so hot and intense, if a drop of it touches a mountain of this world today, it would turn it to dust.

Amongst the food of the dwellers of the Hellfire is the tree of Zaqqum in the lowest level of Hell. Its branches are described like heads of devils. Its vicious fruits severely burn the insides of a sinner's stomach. If a drop of its juice lands on Earth, it will poison the whole Earth and everything it contains.

God the Almighty, the Most Merciful, the Most Compassionate, did not create the Hellfire to just throw people in it nor does he want to. In fact, God asks a rhetorical question in the Holy Koran stating:

"What can Allah gain by your punishment, if you are grateful and believe? And ever is Allah Appreciative and Knowing" (Quran 4:147)

God will get nothing from punishing anyone and he wants reasons not do it. In fact, God states in Holy Quran that He created mankind and Jinn to worship Him, glorify Him, and exalt Him, as He is the Only One worthy of worship, and he states in another verse, from his end, He created mankind so He can show them His Mercy:

"Except whom your Lord has given mercy, and for that He created them...." (Quran 11:119)

One needs to realize that he is a slave, and that God is his Master and one cannot question Him nor His authority nor do they have any right to. A Master can be just and kind or can be unjust and unkind. Allah, the Exalted, is an All-Merciful Master. If one accepts that he is Allah's slave and submits to Him fully, he or she will find that God is The Most Beneficent, the Most Merciful. Only when one submits to His Master, does one find his life become easier and better.

Why would God want to punish an individual when He created him or her with love and mercy in the first place? God wants to warn his servants about Hell now, so one can fix themselves and avoid it to their best of ability. It is best to be informed about the Hellfire now and to recognize its severity, harshness, and how gruesome its punishment is in detail then it is to come across it in the Hereafter unprepared and not knowing. That is a Mercy as God the Almighty could have chosen not to warn one beforehand of the consequences of one's actions.

While God is All-Merciful, He is Also All-Just. He states in the Quran:

> **"Indeed, Allah does not do injustice, [even] as much as an atom's weight..." (Quran 4:40)**

If one commits murder or oppresses an individual, God may punish that person to serve justice to the person killed or oppressed or to serve justice to the family members. God states every soul shall receive their full compensation for the good and evil deeds they commit on the Day of Judgement.

If God allows the oppressors to oppress without punishing them, it would encourage people to oppress and to commit evil which would spread corruption even further. The fear of punishment prevents some people from committing evil. God has also stated he will surely forgive any soul that repents from their sin as He is Extremely Forgiving and Extremely Loving.

There are certain individuals that want to blame God for Hell because they do not want to fix their act, face reality, or be held accountable for their actions. It's important to realize, whether you believe and accept in God and the Hellfire or not, it will not change the reality that God and the Hellfire do exist, and you will soon find out.

> **"O, you who have believed, protect yourselves and your families from a Fire whose fuel is people and stones..." (Quran 66:6)**

JANNAH (PARADISE) ACCORDING TO ISLAM

The term *'Jannah'* is derived from an Arabic word meaning hidden, cover, or concealed, as Jannah is a place which is hidden from sight and covered by trees and plants. Jannah is often translated to mean *'Green Garden.'* Jannah or Paradise is understood to be located in the region of the Seventh Heaven. The English word *'Heaven'* refers to the realm of seven Heavens/Skies that hover above the Earth.

As with other aspects of Islam, Muslims must believe in the concept of Jannah (Paradise) to complete their faith. Jannah is the eternal abode of radiant joy, peace, and bliss in the afterlife, reserved only for faithful and righteous individuals who during their lifetimes believed in the One and Only God—the Ultimate Creator, His Message, and His Prophets and Messengers—and lived righteous lives, following the commandments of God and guarding themselves against evil. It will be the final destination for those entering Paradise, who will dwell there forever and never taste evil or death.

"And Paradise will be brought near [that Day] to the righteous (God-conscious individuals who guard themselves against evil)" (Quran 26:90)

Paradise is exalted, a place of absolute peace and contentment. A person will attain his or her complete fulfillment in this Paradise, where their wishes will be granted with no restrictions. Inhabitants will see only what they desire and listen to sounds that give them pleasure. Unlike the joys of the world we inhabit, the joys and pleasures of Paradise will never fade away and are pure and everlasting.

A person in Paradise will find their company in the righteous, with many families reuniting. Paradise will be free of emptiness, sorrow, hate, boredom, jealousy, handicap, illness, uneasiness, fatigue, disease, hurt, distress, and anxiety. The shade of Jannah will be a shelter of protection and security, and no fear or sadness will afflict its residents.

"And whoever does righteous deeds, whether male or female, while being a believer - those will enter Paradise and will not be wronged, [even as much as] the speck on a date seed" (Quran 4:124)

The bounties, the beauties, and the pleasures of Paradise are so great, so vast, so pure, so astonishing, that it is beyond the abilities of a person's mind to understand; thus, no heart or mind can ever comprehend them. Much like a blind person cannot possibly see or describe colors accurately in this world, a person cannot possibly imagine the delights of Paradise; delights so immense that they have no basis of comparison in the earthly realm. No one will ever be able to fully understand or grasp the true realm of Paradise until they enter its bounds. God's Messenger stated: *'Allah, the Exalted, has said: 'I have prepared for my righteous slaves what no eye has seen, no ear has heard, and the mind of no man has conceived.'* God, the Almighty in his Mercy, has given humanity only glimpses of the descriptions of Paradise in the Holy Quran and narrations of our Prophet Muhammad (Hadith); thus providing an idea of what one can look forward to in Paradise as encouragement and inspiration for one to strive to please their Lord and enter Paradise.

Paradise was created before the creation of mankind by the Almighty, and this ethereal place will never end or cease to exist. The mansions, food, clothing, and jewelry found in Paradise will be far superior to and greater than their counterparts of this world. Unlike the joys and pleasures of this world, the pleasures of Paradise are everlasting. One will never grow tired in Paradise, where delights and pleasures will only increase each time as they indulge in them.

"And no soul knows what has been hidden for them of comfort for eyes as reward for what they used to do" (Quran 32:17)

The first of mankind to enter Paradise will be the last and final Prophet of God, Muhammad peace be upon him; and the first nation to enter Paradise will be his nation, the final nation. Generally, the poor will enter Paradise before the rich. Amongst the first to enter Paradise are Al-Shuhada (the martyrs), the ones who are chaste and proud; and the slaves who worship Allah with devotion, sincerity, and faithfulness towards their Master. Amongst the ones that will enter Paradise first are the 70,000 individuals who will be allowed entrance with no questioning or punishment and according to the narration of our Prophet, arriving with each thousand, will be another seventy thousand, plus three handfuls of the handfuls of our Lord, may He be Glorified.

Paradise consists of seven levels, with each level divided into many stages, levels, and categories. Each level up in Paradise comprises greater joys and pleasures and is more amazing than the level beneath it. The lowest level of Paradise is ten times the size of this whole Universe. The highest level of Paradise is called *Jannat Ul-Firdous*. Our Prophet stated: *'Paradise has one hundred grades, each of which is as big as the distance between Heaven and Earth. The highest of them is Firdaus and the best of them is Firdaus. The Throne is above Firdaus and from its spring forth the rivers of Paradise. If you ask of Allah Glorified and Exalted Be He), ask Him for Firdaus."*

Inhabitants of Paradise from all levels will communicate with one another. Whereas one could visit levels beneath them, one cannot live or enjoy the pleasures of levels higher than he or she inhabits.

Paradise comprise Eight Gates. Each Gate is named and reserved only for individuals who performed specific good deeds. One gate is reserved exclusively for those who fast; another one is meant for those who struggle in the way of God. One gate is for those who pray, and another is for those who give charity. Some will be called to enter from all Eight Gates. The gate at the far right will be for those who will not be held to any accountability. Everyone else will enter Paradise with the rest of their nations, through the other seven gates. The Gates are so vast that the distance between two panels within just one gate of Paradise is that of a distance of forty years' walking—still there will come a time when the ethereal realm gets very crowded.

Before entering Paradise from its gates, one would feel its breeze and inhale its fragrance; both so strong that they can be experienced 40 years away. When the Doors open, upon entering, Angels will greet and congratulate its inhabitants with the greatest of kindness and peace.

"But those who feared their Lord will be driven to Paradise in groups until, when they reach it while its gates have been opened and its keepers say, 'Peace be upon you; you have become pure; so enter it to abide eternally therein'" (Quran 39:73)

The dwellers of Paradise will say:

"And they will say, 'Praise to Allah, who has removed from us [all] sorrow. Indeed, our Lord is Forgiving and Appreciative" (Quran 35:34)

The people of Paradise will live in pure delight without pain and suffering. No one will feel any anger, sadness, sorrow, emptiness, resentment, envy, jealousy, or bitterness towards others; regardless of any differences or disagreements they may have experienced in their life. The hearts of the dwellers of Paradise will be clean and pure. All speech and actions will be good.

"And We will have removed whatever is within their breasts of resentment, [while] flowing beneath them are rivers... "(Quran 7:43)

One would feel absolute safety, tranquility, peace, and contentment in Paradise, facing no worries or concerns. Faces will shine radiant like stars in the sky, some akin to the glow of a full moon. The people of Jannah will praise God not because they are forced to, rather of their own free will. The people of Jannah (Paradise) will never have to use the restroom, spit, or blow their nose. They will have combs made of gold and their sweat will bear the scent of musk. They would wear no hair on their bodies and no beards. The people of Jannah will have beautiful characteristics, their physical forms likening the form of Prophet Adam peace be upon him — 60 feet tall and forever the age of thirty-three. They will have the beauty of Prophet Yusuf peace be upon him and the heart of Prophet Ayyub peace be upon him. The people of Jannah will have the strength of one hundred men of this world.

Paradise will be lined with immense mansions made of gold on top of silver. Rooms upon rooms upon rooms inside these palaces will feature waterfalls falling beneath their rooms. No cracks will mar their facades, nor any repairs will ever be needed. The Soil of Jannah is of pure white musk, and the pebbles are made of pearls, rubies, diamonds, and jewels. The spread carpets in Paradise are culled from soft and colorful silk and are filled with musk, camphor, and amber. The people of Jannah will lean back into the fabrics of luxurious elevated soft couches, and beds with cup holders and comfortable blankets. The beds will be so wide in proximity it would take 500 years to walk through their confines.

The people of Jannah will have a true kingdom which they will control, which will offer whatever they desire. The people of Jannah will have thousands of servants at their command. Paradise will flow forth with rivers of clear, pure water, rivers of milk that never go sour, rivers of pure luscious honey, and rivers of wine that do not intoxicate. Jannah will never be too hot or cold and will always host an environment of the perfect temperature. Jannah has no day or night hours, no sun nor moon, as there will be no need. Paradise contains trees offering shade that seem like they do not cease.

The dwellers of Paradise will eat and drink whatever they wish. If one sees a bird he wishes to eat; it would fall roasted between his hands with no effort on his or her part. Cups will be served to them containing shiny rubies, pearls, and diamonds. Fruits will hang freely from trees and automatically lowered for its inhabits to enjoy whenever they desire.

"[They will be told], "Eat and drink in satisfaction for what you put forth in the days past" (Quran 69:24)

The clothes of Jannah will never wear out or age. The dwellers of Paradise will wear luxurious green silk and will accessorize with jewelry made of diamonds, white pearls, gold, and rubies.

"They will be adorned therein with bracelets of gold and pearl, and their garments therein will be silk" (Quran 22:23)

A crown of magnificence will be placed on heads that would outshine the sun, and residents will be given to wear seventy thousand different clothing adorned with various gems and pearls. One piece of their jewelry would be worth more than this world and everything it contains. The fragrance of the perfume of Paradise will smell so pleasant and strong that the scent would reach up to a distance equal to a thousand years.

To satisfy the natural urge and desire for physical pleasure, virgin spouses will be gifted to be loved and adored.

"Indeed, We have produced the women of Paradise in a [new] creation. And made them virgins. Devoted [to their husbands] and of equal age"
(Quran 56:35-37)

Allah will say to the dwellers of Paradise: *'O' People of Paradise, is there anything else I can give to you?'* The dwellers of Paradise will respond: *'Oh Allah, didn't you beautify our faces, enter us into Paradise, and save us from the Hellfire? You have given us what you have given no one else from your creation.'* Allah will then respond, *'Shall I not give you better than that?'* Then Allah will remove his veil.

Nothing will be more beloved and enjoyable than the vision of Allah, the Glorious. The Ultimate Pleasure one will experience in Jannah is the ability to see their Lord; there is no Greater joy than seeing Allah's Face, and this experience will stand as the Almighty's most precious gift to his servants who entered Paradise.

"[Some] faces that Day will be radiant, Looking at their Lord" (Quran 75:22-23)

Allah will announce to them, *'Death will never come to you again, you will live forever. I am pleased with you today, and I will never be angry at you ever again!'* The inhabitants of Paradise will be able to directly communicate with their Lord, acting as His friend and neighbor.

The dwellers of Paradise will differ in seeing Allah; some will see Him once a week, some will see Him twice a day, etc., depending on the level of Paradise one inhabits. According to our Prophet's narration, the people of Jannah will see God with ease, just like we can see the moon here on Earth.

Ultimately, the life of this world is not meant for one to experience forever. It is a place where one resides temporarily. As a temporary destination, one should prepare themselves to the best of their ability for the next world, their final destination and ever-lasting. It is irrational and illogical for one to become too connected to and engrossed in a temporary world while forgetting and not preparing for their final and eternal destination: the next world.

The descriptions of Heaven found in the Holy Koran, and the Hadith is meant to inspire and encourage one to work harder and become a better person and servant of God. The acts of laziness, procrastination, carelessness, and not using one's intellect can prevent one from entering the abode of never-ending joy and pleasure.

> **"...Say, the enjoyment of this world is little, and the Hereafter is better for he who fears Allah..." (Quran 4:77)**

One should note that the finest and greatest things in this life do not come easy—and neither will the reward of Paradise. One needs to strive to his or her best ability to earn the pleasures of Paradise. God states in his Book:

> **"Race toward forgiveness from your Lord and a Garden whose width is like the width of the Heavens and Earth, prepared for those who believed in Allah and His messengers. That is the bounty of Allah which He gives to whom He wills, and Allah is the possessor of great bounty" (Quran 57:21)**

JESUS CHRIST IN ISLAM

J esus Christ is a Central and revered figure in the Islamic faith. A fundamental pillar of Islam involves the fundamental belief in all of God's Prophets and Messengers, that He has sent down to relay His Message to humanity. Anyone who does not believe in any of God's Messengers or Prophets is considered a disbeliever in Islam. Muslims hold all Prophets of God in high esteem, including Jesus peace be upon him. Muslims love and admire Jesus peace be upon him and will not speak the name of Jesus, or Isa in Arabic, without respectfully adding the words *'peace be upon him'* following the reference.

Aside from Christianity, Islam is the only other religion that requires followers to believe in Jesus Christ. God's last and final Prophet, Muhammad narrated, *'He who bears witness that there is no true god except Allah, alone having no partner with Him, that Muhammad is His slave and His Messenger, that 'Isa (Jesus) is His slave and Messenger, and he (Jesus) is His Word which He communicated to Maryam (Mary) and His spirit which He sent to her, that Jannah (Paradise) is true and Hell is true; Allah will make him enter Jannah accepting whatever deeds he accomplished.'* Jesus Christ is mentioned over 25 times in the Holy Quran.

The mother of Jesus is Mary (Mariam in Arabic). She was a very pious and righteous woman. According to the Quran, she is the holiest and greatest of all women that ever lived. Mary has the great honor to be the only female mentioned by name in the Holy Quran and even has a whole Chapter named after her.

"And [mention] when the angels said, "O Mary, indeed Allah has chosen you and purified you and chosen you above the women of the worlds" (Quran 3:42)

The mother of Mary, Hannah, was at one time a barren woman who longed for a child. She made a vow to God that if He gifted her with a child, then she would consecrate him to His service in the Holiest of all Temples, the Temple of Solomon, to be a scholar or a priest. God answered her prayers and gifted her with a girl child. Hannah was saddened at the child's gender, as usually only male children were given in service. Following her promise to God, she instructed that Mary is raised at the Temple. Her Uncle Zechariah, who was a Prophet of God raised her. As Mary got older, Prophet Zechariah would visit her in her chamber at the Temple, where only he had access, and he would observe that she feasted on the best of foods and cold drinks. He would ask who had delivered these feasts when no one else had keys to the chamber. She then would respond, 'Allah!' She was blessed by miracles from God, even before the birth of Jesus Christ.

According to the Quran, Angel Gabriel walked into Mary's chamber. Terrified that someone had come to harm her or to remove her chastity, she cried out, *'I seek refused from Allah!'* Angel Gabriel responded, *'I am not an enemy, I am Allah's servant and a messenger who came to deliver glad tidings to you, that Allah would bestow upon you a child.'* She replied, 'How can I have a child if I don't have a husband, and no man has touched me?' Angel Gabriel then responded:

"Allah creates what He Wills. If He decrees a thing, He says unto it only: Be! and it is." (Quran 3:47)

Jesus' real name is Esau (Hebrew) or Yeheshua (Classical). The Christians of the West gave the Latin name, Jesus,. The letter 'J' does not exist in Aramaic, so Jesus himself would not recognize the name, Jesus.

Mary gave birth to Jesus in the valley of Bethlehem, away from the people, after which she then returned. The Quran confirms that Jesus was born of a virgin woman. When they saw her with her newborn child Jesus, they said:

"...O Mary, you have certainly done a strange thing. O sister of Aaron, your father, was not a man of evil, nor was your mother unchaste" (Quran 19:27-28)

Mary didn't speak but pointed at her child.

"So she pointed to him. They said, 'How can we speak to one who is in the cradle a child?' [Jesus] said, 'Indeed, I am the servant of Allah. He has given me the Scripture and made me a Prophet. And He has made me blessed wherever I am and has enjoined upon me Prayer and Zakah as long as I remain alive and [made me] dutiful to my mother, and He has not made me a wretched tyrant. And peace is on me the day I was born, and the day I will die, and the day I am raised alive'" (Quran 29-33)

The Quran references the miracles that Jesus performed by the power and will of God, even in his infancy, when he spoke in the cradle to defend his mother's chastity and innocence.

The word *Messiah* is the title of Jesus. The word Messiah comes from the Arabic and Hebrew word *mesaha*, which means to rub, to massage, to anoint. In religious context, the word translates to mean 'the one that has been anointed.' It was common to appoint or anoint a King or Judge of Israel on the head with oil when taking office, as a sign of his inauguration. In the law of previous nations, they would rub a person's head with special water when they converted to their religion. This practice lives on today, in the form of a Baptist ritual. Prophet Jesus was anointed as the next Prophet by his cousin, John the Baptist, the preceding Prophet. Jesus peace be upon him is called by four noble titles: The Messiah, the Messenger of Allah, A Word from Allah, and A Spirit from Allah.

Muslim's belief and understanding of Prophet Jesus stands in accordance with God's final Book, the Holy Quran, and narrations of God's last Prophet, Muhammad peace be upon him. Jesus Christ was a mere prophet of God; whose mission was to confirm the Torah which was revealed before him. He did not come bearing a new law, but only abrogated some laws to make life easier for the Children of Israel—the nation that lived before us. Jesus was sent to teach the same general Message, which was taught by all the previous prophets of God; that we must worship and follow the One God and shun every false god.

God created Jesus Christ without a human father, just as Prophet Adam peace be upon him was born without either a human father or mother; Allah just said Be, and it Was. Declining to call Jesus the son of God is not done to belittle or insult Jesus; instead, it is done to Glorify and Magnify God. Allah is the One and Only, and He is far above having a child or a partner in His divinity.

One should realize that Jesus never claimed to be the son of God, let alone God Himself. Through a careful study of the Bible, one would conclude that Jesus never called himself a god or God's son. Nowhere does it state in the Bible that Jesus proclaimed himself as God. Instead, others made that proclamation after Jesus' departure. Jesus, peace be upon him, only preached the teachings he received from God the Almighty. Prophet Jesus was only a servant and slave of God. He is not the son of God in the sense he was the begotten Son of God, instead; he is—metaphorically -the son of God in the sense that all righteous people are the sons of God. Yet this title is not to be taken literally as many Christians have done in error. There are many individuals labeled 'sons of God' in the Bible including Prophet Jacob, Solomon, and Adam peace be upon them as this was a common saying amongst the children of Israel.

As Jesus Christ grew into adulthood, he began to travel and preach God's Message throughout the land of Palestine to the children of Israel. He taught the scripture that God sent to him, known as the Injeel, which translates to mean 'Good News' or 'Gospel'; confirming the truth of previous Holy Books of God.

"And [I have come] confirming what was before me of the Torah and to make lawful for you some of what was forbidden to you. And I have come to you with a sign from your Lord, so fear Allah and obey me"(Quran 3:50)

To reinforce his Message, God granted Prophet Jesus peace be upon him the ability to perform miracles; such as fashioning birds from clay, then blowing into them to turn them into real birds—healing lepers and the blind, and even resurrecting the dead, all by the will and power of God the Almighty. Never did Prophet Jesus peace be upon him take credit for performing the miracles by himself, without the power of God. According to the Bible, many verses show that Jesus never took credit nor stated that he could perform miracles on his own:

'...All power is given unto me in heaven and in earth' (Matthew 28:18)
'I can of mine own self do nothing ...' (John 5:30)
'...I with the Finger of God cast out devils...' (Luke 11:20)

Prophet Jesus peace be upon him preached and stressed that no deity is worthy of worship except the One true God; and only through Him (the One true God, Allah, which is the unique name of God) can one obtain salvation in the hereafter. Prophet Jesus peace be upon him attracted an inner circle of devoted followers who listened to his teachings with humility; a ring known as the disciples.

Jesus Christ peace be upon him preached the same general Message as the Messengers and Prophets before him. According to the Bible, *'One of the teachers of the law came and heard them debating. Noticing that Jesus had given them a good answer, he asked him, 'Of all the commandments, which is the most important?' 'The most important one,' answered Jesus, 'is this: 'Hear, O Israel: The Lord our God, the Lord is one' (Mark 12:28-29)* Never did Prophet Jesus, nor any other Prophet, preach that God is part of a Trinity.

Because the Children of Israel had gone astray from the straight path of God, Allah, the Glorious, sent them their final Prophet, Jesus Christ, to remind them that this is their last chance to fulfill God's commandments. When Jesus Christ continued to preach God's Message, commanding them to do certain things and to avoid certain things, instead of believing him and following him, they got frustrated by him; turning their backs on him and rejecting him, plotting against him. According to the new testament, a group of hypocritical and self-serving men of the Children of Israelites plotted against Prophet Jesus peace be upon him.

They complained to the Roman authorities, who were pagan idol worshipers who had political power at the time; this because the children of Israel were only a minority. The Children of Israel complained that Prophet Jesus peace be upon him was preaching something new, and they provoked the Romans to rise against him; making the Roman governor believe that the call of Jesus

Christ conveyed direct threats against the Roman power. His people claimed that Jesus Christ was an agitator speaking against the emperor which was not true. The Roman governor issued an order that Prophet Jesus peace be upon him is arrested, then crucified by hanging him on a cross and starving him; a common form of shame killing.

According to the Christian narrative, which Muslims do not believe, the Roman authorities found Jesus Christ, arrested him, then put him on the Roman cross—where he died. They eventually buried him, only to see him resurrected and returned from the dead. He announced to everyone he was the son of God. However, in reality, according to the Holy Quran, God states:

"And [for] their saying (in boast), 'Indeed, we have killed the Messiah, Jesus, the son of Mary, the messenger of Allah.' And they did not kill him, nor did they crucify him; but [another] was made to resemble him to them. And indeed, those who differ over it are in doubt about it. They have no knowledge of it except the following of assumption. And they did not kill him, for certain. Rather, Allah raised him to Himself. And ever is Allah Exalted in Might and Wise." (Quran 4:157-158)

So according to the Holy Quran, they neither killed nor crucified Prophet Jesus peace be upon him; rather, God placed a resemblance of Prophet Jesus peace be upon him on another person to make him like Prophet Jesus. The Christians were differing amongst themselves as to the truth of the matter, as they themselves were in doubt and had no certainty what happened. In all actuality, God rescued His Prophet by raising Prophet Jesus' soul and body up to Himself. The Israelites and the Roman authorities never could harm him, crucify him or kill him; this version of events was only an assumption. According to some Islamic scholars, God punished Judas, the traitor by casting him in a resemblance to Prophet Jesus peace be upon him. So, they crucified him instead, assuming it was Jesus Christ.

According to the New Testament, Jesus Christ returned to his followers. Whereas Christians believe that he returned from the dead, Muslims believe that he never died. His followers were terrified at his reappearance, as they thought he had been crucified. Then Prophet Jesus said: *Look at my hands and my feet. It is I myself! Touch me and see; a ghost does not have flesh and bones, as you see I have' (Luke 24:39)* Jesus Christ then asked for food, so he could eat before them like a human being would, not a spirit or a ghost. After he proved his existence, he told them God had willed him to leave; and that in his absence they should preach and teach his Message and be faithful to God. He promised them finally that another would come after him. Whereas Christians believe that Prophet Jesus was referring to the Holy Spirit in the context of this statement, Muslims believe that his words referenced the Prophet, Muhammad peace be upon him.

Prophet Muhammad peace be upon him is mentioned and prophesied in Scriptures of all major world religions. In the Old Testament, God the Almighty speaks to prophet Moses: *'I will raise up for them (the Israelites) a Prophet like you from among their brethren (the Israelites); I will put my words in his mouth, and he will tell them (the Israelites) everything I command him.' (Deuteronomy 18:18)* This verse is referencing Prophet Muhammad peace be upon him, who came after Prophet Moses and after Prophet Jesus peace be upon them. Prophet Muhammad is also mentioned by name in Song of Solomon Verse 5:16 in Hebrew. The Hebrew word used there is 'Muhammuddim.' The letters 'im' in the end indicates a plural variation of a term that translates to mean respect majesty and grandeur. Without the 'im' suffix, the name would be 'Muhamud'; translated to mean 'the praised one' or 'altogether lovely' in the Authorized Version of the Bible.

Gospel of John 16:12-14 Jesus Christ states: *'I have much more to say to you, more than you can now them bear.'* God did not find it fit for mankind to receive the whole Message of Islam (the way of life of submitting fully to God) at that point, as they would not have been able to bear the Message in its entirety. So, Jesus Christ says: *'But when he, the Spirit of truth, comes, he will guide you into all the truth. He will not speak on his own; he will speak only what he hears, and he will tell you what is yet to come. He will glorify me...'* (Gospel of John 16:12-14) This Spirit of truth is none other than God's last and final messenger of mankind, meant to be followed until the last day. Prophet Muhammad, who came after Jesus Christ, preached the same general Message as Prophet Jesus and every other Messenger and Prophet before him.

After the departure of Prophet Jesus, controversies sparked amongst his followers. They questioned whether the person who returned was really Jesus

Christ. A severe split erupted in the Christian faith, revealing a broad spectrum of opinions regarding Prophet Jesus and his role in the world.

Prophet Jesus was a mighty messenger of God, but he was only a mortal human being. He was born from a mother; he ate and drank; he would sleep and use the bathroom; he suffered pain and emotions. This differentiates him from God the Almighty, as God need not eat, sleep, or drink. He was only a servant and slave of God. The Trinity—the father, the son, and the holy spirit—and the concept that Jesus died for our sins is firmly rejected in Islam.

> **"O People of the Scripture, do not commit excess in your religion or say about Allah except the truth. The Messiah, Jesus, the son of Mary, was but a messenger of Allah and His word which He directed to Mary and a soul [created at a command] from Him. So, believe in Allah and His messengers. And do not say, 'Three'; desist - it is better for you. Indeed, Allah is but one God. Exalted is He above having a son. To Him belongs whatever is in the heavens and whatever is on the earth. And sufficient is Allah as Disposer of affairs" (Quran 4:171)**

God makes it clear in the Quran that the act of ascribing a son to Him, angers him. Ascribing a son to God is beneath the Almighty. God states:

> **"And they say: 'The Most Beneficent (Allah) has begotten a son (or offspring or children)' Indeed you have brought forth (said) a terrible evil thing. Whereby the heavens are almost torn, and the earth is split asunder, and the mountains fall in ruins. That they ascribe a son (or offspring or children) to the Most Beneficent (Allah). But it is not suitable for (the Majesty of) the Most Beneficent that He should beget a son" (Quran 88-92)**

According to the Holy Koran, the one that calls God part of the Trinity is a disbeliever who will face a painful punishment. The Quran states:

> **"They have certainly disbelieved who say, 'Allah is the third of three' And there is no god except one God. And if they do not desist from what they are saying, there will surely afflict the disbelievers among them a painful punishment" (Quran 5:73)**

The Quran then says:

> **"The Messiah, son of Mary, was not but a messenger; [other] messengers have passed on before him. And his mother was a supporter of truth. They both used to eat food. Look how We make clear to them the signs; then look at how they are deluded" (Quran 5:75)**

It's important to mention that Prophet Jesus peace be upon him did not come down with a new Law, nor did he come out to abolish the Old Testament (Torah); instead he came to affirm, teach and preach the previous law, the law of Moses. According to the Holy Koran and the Bible, the Children of Israel were veering away from the laws and disobeying the commandments of God. Prophet Jesus' mission was to confirm the Torah that was previously sent, to render certain things lawful to facilitate life for the Children of Israel and to proclaim and re-affirm the belief in One God. Prophet Jesus peace be upon him was the last in a long line of Messengers sent to the Jewish people.

Prophet Jesus peace be upon him and the Book he came down with, the Injeel (Gospel), was not meant for non-Israelites. According to the Bible, Jesus states: *'I am not sent but unto the lost sheep of Israelites' (Matthew: 15-24)* In another verse, *'These twelve Jesus sent forth, and commanded them, saying, Go not into the way of the Gentiles, and into any city of the Samaritans enter ye not. But go rather to the lost sheep of the house of Israel' (Mathew 10:5-6)*

So, my dear Christian brother and sister, why are you spreading the Gospel to those for whom it was never meant? Jesus states he was sent *'only to the Children of Israel'* and not for everyone else. God has sent another Book after the Gospel—his final Book, the Holy Quran—and his last and final Messenger--Prophet Muhammad peace be upon him — which is meant for our nation, the latest nation to exist on earth until the end of time.

Christians believe that every child is born with the taint of the original sin committed by our parents, Prophet Adam and Eve peace be upon them; a sin committed when disobeying our Creator and eating from the forbidden tree. According to Islam, the notion of the original sin is inconsistent with the concept detailing justice of the Almighty, the All-Merciful, the All-Loving How can God, the All-Just, make an innocent child responsible for or to bear the guilt of a sin committed by a distant ancestor? It is not just for one soul to carry the burden of another, and there is no justice to be found in one person being punished for saving another when they never committed the sin themselves. Islam teaches that everyone is responsible and will be held accountable for their own actions and that everyone is accountable for their own salvation. Salvation only comes from the act of Believing in the One God and following His commandments.

Christians believe that since all men are born in this sinful state, it is necessary that a Christian believes in the atonement; the idea that Jesus Christ died for our sins. However, nowhere in the Bible did Jesus explicitly state that he would die to save mankind from sin. According to the Holy Quran and the Bible itself, one can receive forgiveness of sins from God solely through sincere repentance sought directly from God. If God, the Almighty, wished and willed to forgive humanity, then he certainly could have done so without the need of sacrificing Jesus Christ, his supposedly 'begotten son.'

The idea that all one has to do to attain salvation is to simply believe Jesus Christ died for their sins, without the need of any worship nor the need to follow the Holy Law because Jesus Christ fulfilled it for them, was never preached by Jesus Christ himself—nor is it even in the Bible.

Muslims believe that Jesus is still alive and that he will return to this world in the last days before the Day of Judgement. Muslims believe in the second coming of Jesus Christ. Muslims believe that Jesus Christ will return and preach the true Oneness of God as he has always done, and; he will not preach the trinity. Jesus Christ will prove to the Jews that he never was crucified and will prove to the Christians that they were wrong to ascribe him as divine. Imam Mahdi will be alive at the time of his return, also the time of the Battle of the Great Armageddon that Christians also predict. Muslims will fight on the side of Prophet Jesus peace be upon him, who will be their leader.

According to the Holy Quran, God will ask Prophet Jesus peace be upon him on the day of Judgement:

"...O Jesus, Son of Mary, did you say to the people, 'Take me and my mother as deities besides Allah?' He will say, 'Exalted, are You! It was not for me to say that to which I have no right. If I had said it, You would have known it. You know what is within myself, and I do not know what is within Yourself. Indeed, it is You who is Knower of the unseen. I said not to them except what You commanded me - to worship Allah, my Lord, and your Lord. And I was a witness over them as long as I was among them; but when You took me up, You were the Observer over them, and You are, over all things, Witness. If You should punish them - indeed they are Your servants; but if You forgive them - indeed it is You who is the Exalted in Might, the Wise." (Quran 5:116-118)

Muslims are the true followers of Jesus Christ, following what Jesus Christ preached and taught. To my dear Christian brothers and sisters, it's imperative you research and learn the real Message of Jesus Christ. God, the Almighty has distinguished man above His other creations, by providing him the gift of reason. One would not be considered a rational being if he or she believed in faith without using their intellect, without investigating, rationalizing, analyzing, examining, pondering, and reflecting over what he or she believes and just blindly following their Church and pastor. To my dear Christian brother or sister, take the time to research and think for yourself.

HIJAB

In today's modern vernacular Arabic, the word *'Hijab'* refers to a 'headscarf.' Yet in classical Arabic and the language of the Holy Quran, Hijab refers to a physical curtain, a screen, a partition, or a barrier, that separates one from others when they stood behind a curtain. The one that is being covered by or that is found behind the Hijab is not only covering their head and whole body but also the space around them as they stand behind a curtain, a screen, a partition, or a barrier. According to the Holy Quran, this covering was an extra layer of coverage required to be worn only by Prophet Muhammad's wives.

"...And when you ask [his wives] for something, ask them from behind a partition. That is purer for your hearts and their hearts..." (Quran 33:53)

Not only did the Prophet's wives have to cover their heads and body, but they were required to place a cover or a curtain in front of them to conceal their space when speaking to people other than their *mahram* (a person whom that individual may not marry because of their close blood relationship such as a brother, uncle, nephew, etc..). The Almighty gave additional rules of etiquette pertaining to how one should speak to the wives of the Prophet peace be upon him, dictating that there should stand a physical separation of the noble Women from the common folk, by a barrier that would be opaque, not see-thru, and impenetrable. It provided an extra layer of privacy and is simultaneously a symbol of their high status and dignity. It's essential to express that the classic meaning of the term 'Hijab' in the Holy Quran is not the same as how we understand and use the term today. The wearing of the Hijab was not required by anyone other than the Prophet's wives, as is outlined in the Holy Quran. As for all other Muslim women, the Quran explicitly instructs that women should wear a headscarf in a different verse.

"And tell the believing women to reduce [some] of their vision and guard their private parts and not expose their adornment except that which [necessarily] appears thereof and to wrap [a portion of] their headcovers over their chests and not expose their adornment except to their husbands, their fathers, their husbands' fathers, their sons, their husbands' sons, their brothers, their brothers' sons, their sisters' sons, their women, that which their right hands possess, or those male attendants having no physical desire, or children who are not yet aware of the private aspects of women. And let them not stamp their feet to make known what they conceal of their adornment. And turn to Allah in repentance, all of you, O believers, that you might succeed"
(Quran 24:31)

The Holy Quran uses the word 'Khamar' to refer to a headscarf—that which covers your head. The word Khamar comes from a root word which means to cover something. The word Khamar is similar to the Arabic word Kha'mir which is the word for alcohol, as alcohol impairs one's intellect---one cannot think straight while under the influence of alcohol, as it creates a barrier between the mind and the power of speech and reasoning.

God states in his Book to tell the believing women to wear their Khomar (the plural of Khamar) over their bosom as in throwing their shawl over and cover their chest area. So, besides covering one's chest, the head should be covered too—as the covering of the head is already implied by the use of the word Khomar in this Verse. So, the essentials of the Khamar dictate that the hair is covered, and that cloth cover the chest of the women.

Whereas generally the women of the days of the Prophet peace be upon him would wear headscarves, some of them would push their veils back exposing their chest area. So, God commanded them to cover their chest as well.

Besides covering the head, neck, and chest area, God instructs the believing Muslim woman to throw unto themselves a *Jilbab*—which references a loose outer garment which does not define their body shape and conceal their beauty. This is regarding a situation in which a Muslimah leaves her home or is in the presence of those who are not her Mahram.

"O Prophet, tell your wives and your daughters and the women of the believers to bring down over themselves [part] of their outer garments. That is more suitable that they will be known and not be abused. And ever is Allah Forgiving and Merciful" (Quran 33:59)

Because these Verses in the Holy Quran are explicit and direct, no disagreements or disputes have been posed to this edict by representatives of Islamic scholarship in the past; unless it concerns whether women should also cover their face and feet.

The primary reason why a Muslim woman wears the Hijab can be attributed to a Muslima's belief that her true purpose in life is to worship God the Almighty according to His instructions; as revealed in God's final Revelation to mankind, the Holy Quran and through the teachings of Prophet Muhammad, the final Messenger of God. God made the wearing of the Hijab an obligation and instructed the believing women to wear the head covering in the Holy Quran. So, wearing it is an act of righteousness and an act of obedience to God. A Muslim woman wears the Hijab to gain the pleasure of her Master.

It is the core teaching of Islam that whatever God instructs one to do; it is always best for them to follow the instruction—whether or not one may understand the logic behind it or not. A Muslim woman trusts God and does whatever He instructs her to do, believing that it is best for her, as God knows what's best for her more than she knows herself. God is the Creator of everything and is All-Knowing, All-Wise. Only when she submits to God and obeys His commands, does she reap the benefits and feel tranquility and contentment of life; as she knows that God is pleased with her. By focusing on and submitting to the demands of God, she is set free and is no longer a slave to and prisoner of society's pressures and desires.

"Whoever does righteousness, whether male or female, while he is a believer - We will surely cause him to live a good life, and We will

surely give them their reward [in the Hereafter] according to the best of what they used to do" (Quran 16:97)

Islam stresses the relationship between the body and the mind. In covering her body, a Muslim woman shields her heart from spiritual impurities. A Muslim woman wears the Hijab to uphold Islam's code of modesty. Islam's code of modesty extends to all aspects in one's life, including their dress and how they carry themselves. A Muslim's clothing is an outer manifestation of inner purity, beauty, and humility, as wearing the Hijab embodies moral conduct, character, manners, and speech. A Muslim woman guards her modesty and does not attract unnecessary attention from people, such as a second look, admiration, praise, or sexual attraction from those other than her husband.

Whereas attention from others may boost one's ego for a short period, a Muslim woman acknowledges that this attention might lead to consequences in the long term, such as jealousy from others, envy, competition, affairs, being a bad role model for children, and possibly a marriage break-up; as we see all so often in the west and around the world where dressing immodestly is common. A Muslim woman boasts the trait of *Hayaa'* (*modesty, bashfulness, and a sense of shame*) within her and values her beauty, so she veils herself as the Hijab diverts attention away from her and conceals and protects the Muslimah. God also instructs women to lower their gaze when the opposite gender is present, which shows the trait of Haya.

"And tell the believing women to reduce [some] of their vision and guard their private parts (by being chaste)..." (Quran 24:31)

A Muslima is honored in Islam and Sharia (Islamic Law). Islam elevates the one that covers herself, safeguarding her integrity by not allowing herself to be treated as a sexual object; to be valued and judged externally based solely on her appearance, rather than internally on her righteousness, character, mind, and intellect. A Muslima woman does not desire to adorn her body for men, sexualizing herself to gain attention from those other than her husband.

"...That is more suitable that they will be known and not be abused (molested). And ever is Allah Forgiving and Merciful..." (Quran 33:59)

According to this Verse in the Holy Koran, a Muslima should wear a Hijab and dress modestly so she can be recognized as a Muslima, a woman that is chaste and serious about her modesty. A Muslima sets a standard for herself and sends a message for everyone around her she is not one to sell herself cheap and knows her value, that she is a strong woman with courage, inner strength, endurance, and is a practicing Muslima that would not harm, oppress, or cheat anyone. The Hijab is a shield that helps prevent a Muslima from being a victim of molestation, taunting, humiliation, or teasing. Not only does she wear modest garb to protect herself, but she wears it to protect men and society at large.

Contrary to popular belief, many assume that the Hijab is worn solely to restrain men's illicit desires. It is not the women's responsibility to regulate a man's behavior. Every man is responsible and accountable for their conduct and action. The Holy Qur'an also instructs men to be modest, lower their gaze, guard their modesty, and to handle themselves sensibly in every sphere of their lives. God states:

"Tell the believing men to reduce [some] of their vision and guard their private parts. That is purer for them. Indeed, Allah is Acquainted with what they do" (Quran 24:40)

The Holy Koran instructs men to observe modesty first before addressing women. While many often incorporate the concept of the Hijab with wearing a headscarf, that is only one application of the idea. The Hijab is much more than a head covering, but the overall concept of being modest and humble in other aspects of life as well.

A similar instruction is given in the Bible: *'You have heard that it was said, 'You shall not commit adultery.' But I tell you that anyone who looks at a woman lustfully has already committed adultery with her in his heart' (Gospel of Mathew 5:27-28)*

In the Holy Quran, the Almighty specifically addresses women when He asks them not to show off their adornments, except that which it is proper and easily apparent, and to draw their veils over their bodies due to the physical and biological distinctions that exist between males and females and their modes of attraction to one another. This is evident in today's world, where the disgraceful exposure of sex-appeal is catered overwhelmingly to men as opposed to women—by corporations and industries mindful of how their advertising and selling of products influence their purchasing behavior.

Some feminist movements and media outlets portray the Hijab as a depiction of oppression and slavery of women. While sadly some Muslim women are oppressed in some Muslim countries even though it goes against the teachings of Islam, the overall oppression of women happens in many parts of the world regardless of the oppressor's religion or culture, even if they are atheist in faith. While one can say that a particular government or group of people generally oppress women, it is not truthful to say that Islam oppresses women. No Islamic laws oppress women, Islam states women have every right to a decent life without facing aggression or abuse of any sort.

If women were indeed granted their God-given rights, oppression would not exist in the manner it does today. Unfortunately, Islam is not being practiced as it should be—even in Muslim land. Islam honors women; yet sadly across the globe, Muslim women fall victim to cultural aberrations that have no place in this beautiful, perfect faith.

A Muslim woman who covers her hair or places her religion above worldly pursuits is sometimes labeled oppressed; but in reality, oppression is not defined by a piece of material on one's head, but by a weakening of the heart and mind. Liberation means freedom, but not freedom to do as one pleases. Freedom must never come at the expense of oneself or others. When a Muslim woman fulfills the role for which she was created, to find God, build a relationship with, and follow His guidance and commands, not only is she liberated—but is empowered and honored. She is liberated and freed from the shackles of society, the pressures of society, and the unrealistic stereotypes and images dictated by the media. Muslim women who chose to cover their hair and dress modestly view the act as a right, and not a burden.

The concept of Hijab is not a concept unique to Islam. Both Christianity and Judaism share many beliefs, including covering one's hair in public with a veil. It was the custom of Jewish women and Catholic Nuns to go out in public with their heads covered. As recently as 40-50 years ago, it was unheard of for a

Christian woman to go to church without covering her head nor wearing a long skirt.

In fact, the concept of a female head covering is found in the Bible stating a woman must cover her head and if she shows her head uncovered, she dishonors her head—and should have her head shaved off: *'But every woman that prayeth or prophesieth with her head uncovered dishonoureth her head: for that is even all one las if she were shaven. For if the woman be not covered, let her also be shorn: but if it be ma shame for a woman to be shorn or shaven, let her be covered'* (1 Corinthians: 11: 5-6)

Unlike related passages found in the Holy Qur'an, Paul in this verse presented the veil as a sign of man's authority. A woman wearing her headscarf, in his view, should do so to show her subordination to a man. This sexist view of women covering their heads reflects the influence of certain individuals in the west, who think the Hijab is oppressive and a symbol of inferiority and degradation. This is because they subconsciously are reacting to the Judea-Christian concept of the veil which is the symbol of woman's subjection to her husband. This is not the case in Islam at all.

The concept of the Hijab comes with necessary conditions which should be followed by Muslima women. The terms are that the whole body, except for the face and hands, should be covered, and by clothing that is loose, not tight, and not transparent. The dress should not attract attention or accentuate the body, should not be perfumed, and should not resemble clothing worn by men or unbelievers—nor should it be overly elegant nor ornate.

God has given an exception to this rule to those who are no longer capable of bearing children, who no longer desire marriage or sexual relations, and who cannot excite the passions of men. These ladies do not need to cover themselves to the same degree as other women do. They are allowed to remove their outer garment, known as a Jilbab in Arabic.

"And women of post-menstrual age who have no desire for marriage - there is no blame upon them for putting aside their outer garments [but] not displaying adornment. But to modestly refrain [from that] is better for them. And Allah is Hearing and Knowing" (Quran 24:60)

The Prophet of God peace be upon him praised modest women, who guard their chastity, and the beauty bestowed upon them by God. Prophet Muhammad peace be upon him also cursed those women that display and flaunt their beauty in public, stating that those women will not smell the fragrance of Paradise. Our Prophet peace be upon him has warned us that towards the end of time, women will exist who are dressed yet naked, he warned us of women who will turn away from righteousness and will be inclined to do evil, leading others astray—including their husbands.

To my dear believing sister, let not the whispers of shaitan (satan) mislead and misguide you. And let not satan drag you from your Creator, the All-Merciful, All-Loving. You need to recognize that you are not in a position to negotiate your faith, what you should accept and what you should decry. You need to submit fully and willingly. And realize, my dear sister, that you are blessed and honored to be amongst the people of La Ala Ila Allah (There is no deity worthy of worship except Allah). Do not procrastinate, as your death can occur at any moment, bringing with it an end to the test of your faith and actions.

The act of not wearing a Hijab or not dressing modestly is a sin, but to justify your actions is much worse. When you are honest with yourself and will admit your transgressions, you gain the chance for repentance, change, and forgiveness. Feeling guilty of sin is the first step of repentance.

Like any other act of worship, the act of dressing modestly and wearing Hijab will require faith, sacrifice, discipline, and patience. Dressing modestly strengthens the relationship between you and your Lord.

To my dear sister who is struggling through her journey of Hijab, strengthen your prayer rituals and connection with God and His Holy Book. Supplicate to Him and beg for His Help. Pray and enhance your relationship with Him, as these acts will keep you away from sins and unlawful acts—giving you the power you need to resist evil elements. Take the first step now and never give up on your quest for faith.

Wear the Hijab for the sake of God alone and ignore the outside noise, ignore people's stares and comments, and realize that this journey is worth the struggle. Realize that pleasing people is a goal you can never achieve and that pleasing your Creator is the road to contentment and peace. Our Prophet peace be upon him narrated: *'Whoever seeks Allah's pleasure by incurring the wrath of the people, Allah will suffice and protect him from the people. And whoever seeks the people's pleasure by Allah's wrath, Allah will entrust him to the people.'* Surround yourself with righteous, practicing sisters, realizing that you are too precious to be on display for each man to see. And realize, my dear sister, that you and your believing sisters are the last true representatives of femininity on this Earth.

CONVERTING TO ISLAM

The one that converts to Islam embraces the folds of this faith because they chose to voluntarily submit and surrender to the Will of God, in exchange for the ultimate acquisition of peace and contentment in this life and the Hereafter. The one that is converting accepts the Islamic belief that to achieve true peace of mind and surety of the heart, one must submit to the Ultimate Creator, the One True God, and live according to His Divinely revealed Laws. The one that converts comes to the understanding that no one is worthy of his or her worship and veneration except the One True Creator, the ultimate Creator, the Creator of this World and everything in it. He realizes that the only true purpose of his or her life to find God, build a relationship with Him, and follow His commandments.

The one that is converting realizes that God the Almighty, would not leave him or her in darkness without guiding and showing them how He wants them to live. So, He (God) chose Messengers and Prophets throughout history to send to different nations at different times to communicate His Message to humanity, to show how one should live, and to teach humanity about Himself. These prophets came with glad tidings, stating that whoever Worships the One God with no partners and lives a righteous life while obeying God's commands will enter Paradise eternally; and whoever worships other than Allah and does not follow God's commandments will enter the hellfire.

Islam is not a new religion but embodies the eternal act of submitting to the will of God. It is the only acceptable religion in the sight of God. Islam is the true natural religion and offers the same Message revealed through the ages to all of God's Prophets and Messengers.

The one that is converting to Islam realizes that Islam will change his or her life for the better and that Islam will provide the light to guide them in their life and grant them true salvation from the eternal hellfire.

The one that searches for his purpose in life, and for his Creator, and is sincere and curious to learn the Truth, that person will eventually be guided to the Truth by the Will of God, and by His Mercy, Love, and Justice. God guides those whom He Wills and Pleases.

My dear brother or sister, if you have the desire to be a Muslim and have a firm conviction and belief that Islam is the true religion of God, then you are ready to embrace the folds of Islam. In Islam, every action begins with one's intention, so start by setting your intention in your heart to embrace Islam for the sake of God alone. It's highly recommended that you first take a bath or shower to symbolically purify and cleanse yourself of your past life and your past sins. It's also recommended that you wear suitable clothes on the day of your conversion.

Unlike other religions, the act of converting to Islam does not involve any rituals, ceremonials, nor baptisms. All one has to do is declare the testimony of faith, which is known as the *Shahada* in Arabic, or the *declaration of faith* in English, which is the first of five pillars of Islam. These two statements encapsulate all the beliefs of Islam:

ورسوله عبده محمدا أن وأشهد   الله إلا إلـه لا أشهد أن
'I bear witness that there is no deity worthy of worship except Allah,
and I bear witness that Muhammad is his servant and messenger.'

You can state this phrase in privacy by yourself or in public with witnesses, which is recommended as you could have help from others with the accuracy of the pronunciation of the wording in Arabic. The testimony of faith is recommended and often done publicly, in a Mosque or gathering.

You testify, acknowledge, and express you are fully convinced that there is no deity worthy of worship and veneration other than Allah. Allah is the unique name of God; the ultimate Creator. You acknowledge that there is Only One God who is the Sustainer, the Creator, who is in control of all matters and all things, who has no partners, no children, nor associates. He is the Most-High, Most-Merciful, All-Knowing, All-Wise, All-Seeing, All-Hearing, He is the First; He is the Last.

You also testify and acknowledge that Muhammad peace and blessings be upon him is the last and final messenger of God, who was sent to relay the same general Message as the prophets before him. He is the best example and role model for humanity, a slave and worshipper of Allah and should not be wrongly worshipped like past Prophets—who were only human messengers of God, and not God himself.

After you complete your testimony of faith, you are now officially Muslim. As a new convert, you do not need to be burdened by your past sins committed before your acceptance, as all of your past sins would be wiped clean, and you would start with a clean slate—as free of sin as a newborn child. Not only that, but all of your past sins would be converted to good deeds. You should attempt to the best of your ability to keep your slate clean as much as possible and do as many good deeds as you can.

As a new convert, make a lot of supplications to God, asking him to continue to guide you to the straight path and lead you to Paradise and everything else you desire—in this world and the Hereafter.

You should gradually continue learning more about Islam and practicing it by performing your five mandatory ritualized prayers that Muslims perform daily. You should not try to learn all aspects of the faith at once, as that might overwhelm you. Instead, continue to learn and grow your faith over an extended period. It's highly recommended that you find a local Mosque or local Islamic community and attend their gatherings, seek Muslim support, and make new friends. You should also give charity and fast in the month of Ramadan, both of which are mandatory upon every Muslim.

For those who are still unsure whether or not they should convert to Islam, they can pray to God without explicitly naming him; praying out and saying, *'Oh you who created me, please guide me to the truth'* Then continue to research and look further at the overwhelming evidence and proofs that Islam offers to affirm its existence and validity. Do not procrastinate, and do not take this matter of faith lightly, as you are not guaranteed tomorrow! Your test your life, can end at any moment. Realize, my dear brother or sister, that you did not come to this passage by random or chance. Your Creator guided you here.

May your journey to the answer, and the truth be pleasant and successful

Everyone is encouraged to visit the various posts and videos featured on The Sincere Seeker Blog on https://www.thesincereseeker.com or on The Sincere Seeker's YouTube Channel. People are also encouraged to subscribe to The Sincere Seeker newsletter and YouTube Channel, to be notified when a new post or video is available for review.

For questions or comments, contact The Sincere Seeker at *hello@thesincereseeker.com*

Made in the USA
Las Vegas, NV
12 February 2021